MOBILE LEARNING MINDSET

THE TEACHER'S GUIDE TO IMPLEMENTATION

CARL HOOKER

International Society for Technology in Education
PORTLAND, OREGON • ARLINGTON, VIRGINIA

Mobile Learning Mindset
The Teacher's Guide to Implementation
Carl Hooker

Editor: *Emily Reed*
Production Manager: *Christine Longmuir*
Copy Editor: *Kristin Landon*
Cover Design: *Brianne Beigh*
Book Design and Production: *Kim McGovern*

Library of Congress Cataloging-in-Publication Data available

First Edition
ISBN: 978-1-56484-376-0
Ebook version available

Printed in the United States of America

ISTE® is a registered trademark of the International Society for Technology in Education.

About ISTE

The International Society for Technology in Education (ISTE) is the premier nonprofit organization serving educators and education leaders committed to empowering connected learners in a connected world. ISTE serves more than 100,000 education stakeholders throughout the world.

ISTE's innovative offerings include the ISTE Conference & Expo, one of the biggest, most comprehensive ed tech events in the world—as well as the widely adopted ISTE Standards for learning, teaching and leading in the digital age and a robust suite of professional learning resources, including webinars, online courses, consulting services for schools and districts, books, and peer-reviewed journals and publications. Visit iste.org to learn more.

About the Author

Carl Hooker has been involved in education since graduating from the University of Texas in 1998. He has been in a variety of positions in both Austin Independent School District (ISD) and Eanes ISD, from first grade teacher to virtualization coordinator.

Hooker is now director of innovation and digital learning at Eanes ISD. He is also the founder of the learning festival iPadpalooza (http://ipadpalooza.com). As director, he uses his background in both education and technology to bring a unique vision to the district and its programs. During his tenure, Eanes has jumped into social media, adopted the Google Apps for Education, and started to build a paperless environment with Google Docs. Hooker helped spearhead the Learning and Engaging through Access and Personalization (LEAP) program, which put 1:1 iPads into the hands of all K–12 students at Eanes.

Hooker has been a part of a strong educational shift with technology integration. From his start as a teacher to his current district technology leadership role, he has always held one common belief: Kids need to drive their own learning. He realizes the challenges in our current public educational institutions and meets them head-on. His unique blend of educational background, technical expertise, and humor makes him a successful driving force for this change. Hooker also works as a keynote speaker and consultant through his company HookerTech, LLC.

Contents

Preface

In January 2010, Steve Jobs took the stage at a major Apple event to announce the creation of a device that was in between a laptop and a smart phone. When he announced the iPad, the reviews were mixed. Wasn't this something that had been tried before, even with Apple's MessagePad (http://en.wikipedia.org/wiki/MessagePad)? How was this going to work in mainstream society when it was bigger and bulkier than a phone and didn't have the keyboard of a laptop?

At the time of the announcement, I was a virtualization coordinator for the district. The technology director (my boss at the time) looked at me with wonder when I showed my excitement over this announcement. "This is going to change the face of education," I told him. His response: "I bet they don't sell even a million of them. It's like a crappy version of a laptop, only you can only do one thing at a time on it. It doesn't even have a USB port!"

In retrospect, I should have taken that bet, as Apple went on to sell a million in pre-orders alone. Flash forward a few more months. On April 2nd I was promoted to the role of Director of Instructional Technology. The very next day the first-generation iPad began to be sold in U.S. stores. I point this all out to show that even with all the prep work and sweat necessary for a successful device deployment, some synergy is also required.

As director of instructional technology, I was taking over a dying role of sorts. Many districts were cutting the position at that time in Texas, and some felt it was a "nice to have" more than "a need to have" position. Knowing that going in, I made it one of my personal missions to erase the thought from the minds of the purse-string holders that my position could ever become obsolete. In fact, I set out to do the exact opposite: make them think they couldn't function successfully without it.

A big part of any leadership position is assessing risks. With the announcement of the iPad, my mind immediately went to education. How could these devices help students personalize their own learning? How would they enhance engagement and the learning experience of students? Are those gains in engagement and personalization enough to justify giving every student one of these devices?

These questions and many others went through my mind and those of many of the leaders in my district in the months that followed. Ultimately, in the fall of 2010, our district took the first steps toward providing 1:1 mobile devices. Whereas some districts chose to make big splashes with their first deployment, our initiative started with a forward-thinking librarian (Carolyn Foote) purchasing six first-generation iPads for students and teachers to check out.

Enter the second synergistic event. A group of leaders including myself made a trip to Cupertino, California, for an executive briefing on Apple's ideas for iPads in education. Before lunch of the first day, the Westlake High School principal leaned over and said to us, "We need one of these for every student." At that time, iPads were considered purely consumptive devices—a nice way to read a book or take notes, but nothing in the way of creativity. That trip to Apple's headquarters changed all of that for those in the room, even those who had been skeptical.

When we returned, we went on to expand the pilot to around 70 different users. From special education students to principals to high school AP teachers, we had as many key stakeholders as possible get their hands on this device to put it through its paces. At this point the iPad 2 had just launched and had a lot more functionality for creativity than its predecessor, namely the addition of a camera.

The pilot went on to expand into Westlake High School the following fall, and eventually reached all 8,000 Eanes ISD K–12 students by the spring of 2013. Here's an early blog post right after launch of the pilot on the EanesWifi site: http://eaneswifi.blogspot.com/2011/09/wifi-pilot-gets-started.html. Along the way, we've seen the highs and lows of having a device for every student, especially one as nimble and easy-to-use as an iPad.

The Mobile Learning Mindset series chronicles that journey from the perspective of six different components. Each component was key to making the initiative as successful as it's become, and as you'll learn, they are all intertwined with each other. This series is not specifically geared toward a 1:1 or Bring Your Own Device (BYOD) initiative. It's meant to be read as a handbook for any teacher, leader, or parent who is involved with a school that is using mobile device technology in the classroom.

The first book goes into detail about what district leadership can and should do to make a mobile device initiative successful. Having a strong, clearly defined goal and vision for a district that's well-communicated is an important part of the process. From the superintendent to the school board to the district and campus level administrators, all need to be singing the same lyrics in the song of 1:1, or else it may fall flat.

The second book in the series is specifically focused on campus leaders and how they can support and showcase the initiative at the campus level. The book discusses the role the campus leader plays in terms of parent communication, teacher expectations, and highlighting student-led projects in the classroom.

The third book in the series focuses on diving into ideas and best practices for professional development around a 1:1. I've seen many a district, including my own, continue the previous practices of professional development of a "sit n' get" style of learning, all the while preaching about how the students need to be the center of the learning. This book focuses on how to make that shift in your organization and ideas on how to make learning more engaging for your staff.

This fourth book is an in-depth look at how mobile devices affect the classroom and what teachers can do both right out of the box and further down the road to sustain a successful student-led learning environment. Using mobile devices as just a substitute for a textbook is a waste of money. These devices are multimedia studios of creation, but often that use is restricted by the classroom teacher. This book uses models such as SAMR and tools that a teacher can use right away to shift the way learning takes place from a traditional classroom to a mobile classroom.

One major part of a mobile learning initiative is keeping community parents educated on the ins and outs of having mobile devices around the home, which is the focus of my fifth book. Part of the disruptive effect that mobile devices have on learning also affects the home. Parents are now facing dilemmas of social media, cyberbullying, and digital footprints that their parents never had to deal with. This book will serve as an instruction manual of sorts for parents raising kids in the digital age.

Last, none of this is possible without proper technical support. From infrastructure to break-fix scenarios, having a technology services department on-board is vital. The final book in the series is centered around that support. Technology changes so frequently that it is nearly impossible to create a book that has all the latest trends and gadgets. This book will focus on some necessary components of supporting a 1:1 mobile device initiative, as well as how to work with leaders, teachers, trainers and parents on making the initiative a success.

Each book has a similar structure. Included among the chapters is one on "top 10 things not to do," an interview with an area expert in that book's particular focus, and chapters dedicated to ideas and strategies for interacting with all the other "players" in a mobile device initiative. In other words, how does a district leader support his/her teachers in this new environment? What expectations should the campus administrator have for his/her staff in terms of professional development? And conversely, how can professional development support those expectations?

All of these six components are parts of the very complex, constantly evolving machine that is a mobile learning initiative. Each plays its part, and each requires different amounts of attention and support from the other parts in order to work efficiently. Neglecting one of these components will result in the other parts having to work harder and could ultimately cause the machine to break down. My hope is that if you use this book series to learn how all the parts work, your own mobile learning machine will be a thing of beauty for your students. After all, their learning and their future is the ultimate reason to do something as bold as an initiative using mobile devices in the classroom.

Good luck, and thank you for being a part of this mobile learning revolution!

—*Carl Hooker*

INTRODUCTION

"I'm not very tech savvy"

This is a statement I have heard ever since I started teaching back in 1998. At that time, technology was creating HyperStudio stacks on colorful flavors of iMacs. Although I didn't have a technology background out of college, I was open to trying new things and figuring out ways to solve problems. At one point late in my teaching career, a teacher approached me and offered to watch my class. When I asked her why, she said "I'm not very tech savvy, but I'm trying to do something with PowerPoint, and I can't figure out how to make it work."

I realized at that moment that teachers have the power within them to try new things as long as they feel some level of support. That support can come from administration, parents, peers, or even students. Many of the things I tried in my classroom failed. When I added technology to the equation, the opportunity for failure seemed to increase exponentially. However, I didn't stop trying.

When we first started down the road of our L.E.A.P. initiative (then called the "Westlake Initiative For Innovation" or WIFI Project), our state had recently reduced the amount of funds allocated for public schools. Although we didn't lose any teachers due to these cuts, it did mean losing more than half of the support staff we had in place for technology integration. So on the heels of launching our first ever 1:1 pilot, we now had to figure out how to help teachers with the integration of a mobile device in their classroom with less support than they were used to. Add to that, the reduction of their extra planning period and we were forced to commit two cardinal sins: removing support and reducing time.

Classroom teachers in our district had a couple of options. They could abandon the use of the new mobile devices because of fear, lack of time, and lack of support. The other option was to persevere and take a risk in the hopes of engaging students and increasing their motivation to learn and dig deeper into a particular subject.

Anytime you commit funds into an initiative, you must make sure you have both a culture that believes in it (see the first two books in this series) and the support and training (see book number three) to make it happen. But all of this is dependent on the classroom teacher willing to invest their time and energy into meaningful integration of the devices into their classroom and adapting their learning environment to make learning truly student-driven.

How to Use This Book

This book is broken down into various chapters that will serve as both a guide and a resource for teachers depending on the state of your mobile learning initiative. The structure of the chapters in this book will mirror the structure of the other books in the series, though the content will differ.

The first three books really tackle both the "why" and "how" of mobile learning. Getting leadership on board with encouraging a learning culture and having professional learning that supports the teacher is key. This book is all about the classroom, and the leader of that classroom experience for students is the teacher. In Chapter 1, we tackle the idea of moving learning from the front of the room toward the center of the room, and how mobile learning can help with that.

Chapter 2 is focused on the top 10 things *not* to do as a teacher with a mobile device initiative in place. Modeling, communicating with parents, classroom management, and feeling isolated are a big part of things *not* to forget or address. This chapter begins to outline many of the other chapters throughout the book when it comes to ideas and strategies for integrating mobile learning into your classroom.

Chapter 3 is an interview with middle school math teacher Cathy Yenca (@mathycathy on Twitter). Not only is Cathy a member of the Apple Distinguished Educator class of 2013 (same as me!), but in our school district, she also champions the meaningful use of technology and mobile devices on a daily basis in her class. I've had the pleasure of seeing many of her lessons in action, and she has some great advice for fellow teachers when it comes to mobile learning.

The middle chapters cover various intricacies involved in having mobile devices in your classroom. Chapter 4 tackles probably the most commonly raised issue: how to manage a classroom where every student has access to the internet and thousands of apps. Chapter 5 discusses the learning environment and what role that plays in the use of mobile devices for learning and collaboration.

In Chapter 6, I discuss the SAMR model and what it looks like when integrated into your lessons. In this chapter, I also offer ways to relieve some of the pressures that teachers face with the multitude of tests and the many changes that come their way on a daily basis. Doing a few things a little differently can go a long way toward making a lasting impression on student outcomes.

One of the small changes that can have great impact is the focus of Chapter 7. Formative assessments become so much more manageable and powerful with the use of mobile devices. I not only discuss the research and thinking behind formative assessments, I also give some of my favorite go-to tools to use for assessment that can be used on any device and without a student login.

Chapter 8 provides an overview of a concept I call "the Mobile Learning Quadrant" (or MLQ). This is really in some ways a culmination of all the chapters before it when it comes to the use of space, time, collaboration, and content creation within the classroom. Being aware of these things in your own classroom may well guide you toward some new ideas for integration that you hadn't considered. You might also find that many of these ideas you have already implemented in some form or fashion.

In our final two chapters, I tie together the other components of this book series and how they interact with teachers and the classroom environment. Professional learning needs to be available to support your growth and development as a teacher. The campus and district leaders need to support your ability to try new things as well as create a supportive learning organization. The parents in your community can be an important part of making the mobile learning in and outside of your classroom a success. And finally, getting the technology department on board with your ideas and garnering their support of technology in your classroom is key.

"Easter Eggs"

According to Wikipedia, an Easter egg is "an inside joke, hidden message, or feature in an interactive work such as a computer program, video game or DVD menu screen." Why can't we also have these in books? In this book, I've hidden several Easter eggs that you'll have to uncover and discover. Some are buried in words, others in images. How do you reveal them? If you are reading this book in its paper form, you'll need to download the Aurasma app (www.aurasma.com/#/whats-your-aura) and find the trigger images to unlock the Easter eggs. Find and follow the "MLM Channel" to make it all work. Instructions can be found here: http://mrhook.it/eggs. Happy hunting!

CHAPTER 1

CHANGING THE CENTER

The role of the teacher has evolved in many ways through the years. In 370 B.C., Greek philosopher Socrates popularized a version of teaching that has stood the test of time. His lecture formats were designed so that one person was the sole source of all knowledge and information. This single person would distribute "learning" by passing on knowledge, thoughts, and philosophies to those who were within earshot. The skill of listening, and interpreting what was said, was crucial to becoming a successful student during this time. Learning happened in isolation, with a few select students having access to the knowledge-bearer and working independently to comprehend what they had learned. That model was effective at the time, but innovation through the centuries has made information and knowledge much more freely available.

The first significant innovation to affect education and knowledge dissemination came in the 1400s when Gutenberg invented the printing press. All of a sudden, information from a single source could be replicated on a large scale and distributed to the masses. The relationship of teacher and pupil shifted from passing down information to more of a master-apprentice relationship. With information in book form becoming widely available, the teacher needed to make sure the student not only understood the information, but also knew how to apply it in some form. Reading became the most essential skill for any student hoping to succeed in the future world. Teaching style was still largely stylized in the Socratic-lecture method, because students needed help decoding exactly what they were reading in books and how to take the information from a knowledge level to higher understanding and application. (See the lower level of Bloom's taxonomy.)

We are now in the midst of a second significant innovation in education with the introduction of mobile devices and the internet in classrooms. Information has now become nearly ubiquitous, accessible by all with a mobile phone and a 3G connection. However, if you look in the classroom, most of the same lecture- and book-focused formats remain. This shift in knowledge has not translated to a different teaching approach. Although listening and reading remain important skills in the classroom, in order to achieve higher-order thinking skills, our students must move past the application phase of their learning. Essential skills for this next generation of learners now includes the ability to think critically about real-world problems and come up with creative solutions. Students must be able to work both independently and collaboratively to effectively communicate their understanding. Continuing to teach in a lecture-style format, day in and day out, doesn't allow for this higher level of interaction and creativity. As you'll see in the following chapters of this book (and yes, there is some irony that this is in book format), there are many different ways of shifting this style of learning from teacher-centric to student-driven.

Making the Shift

To anyone who was trained in the Madeline Hunter (http://mrhook.it/hunter) model of instruction, shifting to something more project-based may seem like letting go of the reins of the horse. The Hunter model of lesson design emphasizes knowledge repetition (sometimes called "drill and kill") for students. In an era where standardized test scores can make or break a school, this model might seem to be the most appropriate for educating our students. But there is one major flaw with this method of teaching: it's highly prescriptive. The only questions asked are those in the plans, and the goal of every lesson is to get to the end. When students get through the standards and expectations, they are then given directions or modeled on what to do next. When I taught using this method, I would often find 22 examples of student work that looked strangely similar to my model example.

God forbid a student should ask a question that wasn't exactly aligned with the objectives of the lesson, or maybe seek some deeper understanding. There was a finite amount of time to make it through this type of instruction, and rarely did that allow for differentiation, with the exception of "independent practice" time. For me, shifting off of this method required taking a long hard look in the mirror. Were students truly learning with this method of instruction? Or were they just able to regurgitate what I had taught them on the test?

Late in my teaching career I began to see the errors in this method of instruction. In 2003, which would be my last year in the classroom as a full-time teacher, I decided to abandon this method for the most part. I was teaching first grade at the time, and rather than going through a standard scope and sequence, I decided to work with others on my team and play to our strengths as well as to the interests of the students. We designed our lessons to be much more centered around student outcomes rather than knowledge regurgitation. We expanded our activities from a single stand-alone math activity to ones that would encompass multiple layers of subject matter. It was essentially inquiry-based learning before that term became commonplace.

By the time we entered the final nine weeks of that school year, my students had reached all the goals and checkpoints required of first graders in the state of Texas. The problem? I still had nine weeks of school left. Although I would have loved to give them a head start on second grade, I knew that wouldn't be fair to all the other teachers at my grade level, and it would makes life tougher for the next-level teachers.

We had just received two major pieces of technology in our school that I had been dabbling with. One was a digital projector (there were only two in the building back then, and they were about the size of a small aircraft carrier). This meant the days of coming home with smeared overhead marker on my hand were over, but it also meant that I could present information and ideas in a much more dynamic way. The other major new piece of technology were called COWs (Computers on Wheels). These COWs had 12 Apple iBooks in them, which I could use to supplement the four Compaq desktop computers I already had in my class.

Having access to this technology meant I could do some different things with my students and perhaps teach them some computer literacy along the way (which would actually lead to my next career as a computer lab teacher). I decided to get out of the way and let the students choose what they would like to learn about in greater depth for the final weeks of the year. I set some parameters: regardless of topic, the learning must contain some portion of writing, math, science, and social studies. I also made the students present their work in a capstone demonstration at the end to their parents, peers, and myself. Finally, I insisted that they use technology for some part of their project (believe me, this part wasn't hard to sell).

Students picked topics from sharks to tornadoes to, for one particular student who was obsessed with the actress, Rachel Weisz. Along with their technology component, students needed to create some sort of demonstration or model to show what they had learned. When all the final projects were finished, I asked the students to evaluate and reflect on all they had learned. I was amazed at the higher level of thinking that was taking place in my classroom. The scary thing was, I actually felt like I wasn't doing that much "teaching." Aside from my many hours of preparatory research and setup, the students were doing most of the work. I made sure to find one "treasure" to award each student that aligned with their work, such as a shark's tooth, a book about tornadoes, and, yes, even an autographed picture of Rachel Weisz.

I had effectively made the shift from teacher-centered to student-driven learning, and I hadn't even realized it. Years later, many of these students (now in their teens) found me on Facebook and posted several messages exclaiming how much they enjoyed my class and the capstone passion projects they had ended the year with. My colleagues, noticing the risk-taking and innovation I was attempting in my classroom, also rewarded by making me the Teacher of the Year on campus.

Are Colleges Preparing Us to Teach in the 21st Century?

I recently guest-lectured a group of student teachers from a local university. I say lecture in the loosest of terms, because in actuality I tried to mimic the role of the educator in the modern classroom. I made sure the students were doing some sort of collaborative work in the form of an Interactive Learning Challenge (see Book 3 for more on those), and they not only presented their outcomes, they had to reflect on the process.

To my amazement, not all the students in the room were very comfortable with this approach. They had become accustomed to playing the "game" of school even through college, which meant sitting back and regurgitating content to some extent. The occasional class would include some level of dynamic discussion or interaction, but actually working on digital projects as a group in class was rare.

What was more amazing than their lack of interest in doing something fun and interactive was the fact that many of them had no clue about how to meaningfully use technology, much less mobile devices, in the classroom environment. I asked the group what kind of technology tools they used on a regular basis for learning and received a lot of blank stares. "Microsoft Office?" one student feebly suggested. They had missed the point. So when I asked them what type of technology tools they used in their lives on a regular basis, they began to share more freely. Instagram, Facebook, Pinterest, Google (the search engine more than the apps), Twitter, and a few others were mentioned.

I asked them if they ever used these tools in an educational setting, and many of them shook their heads. Some even laughed.

I then decided to let them in on a little secret.

"When you enter our schools, we assume you not only know how to use this technology as a 'digital native,' but also that you'll be the most effective in integrating it."

Again ... blank stares.

A few months later I encountered another group of student teachers. This group was going through our district orientation. My part in the orientation was to go over the do's and don'ts of social media and technology use in our district. As they walked into the room, I took a quick glance at the list of names on the sign-in sheet. While the superintendent shared some messages about school culture and the like, I did some searching of their names on Google. Within seconds I had my first "hit."

When my part came, I had all of the student-teachers take out their phones to play my version of Responsible Use Guidelines via Kahoot! (Learn more about Kahoot! in Chapter 7.)

In the middle of the game, I got to a question about what to post and not to post on social media. Although all the students had gotten it right, I told them that when they walked in I had done some quick research on each of them. Immediately I noticed some nervous shifting in the room.

"Maggie, I noticed you posted some interesting pictures on Instagram. Let's take a look at one." I then opened up a tab that revealed the student at an art museum taking pictures of works of art. I could sense the relief wash over her face and with good reason. Two pictures before that picture was a photo of her in a pool wearing a bikini and holding a beer. I chose not to show that picture, but she and all the other student teachers in the room became instantly aware that their lives were about to change when they entered education (or any other field for that matter). I asked them if anyone at the university level had ever spoken to them about this.

Again ... blank stares.

I share these examples with you, the teacher reading this book, to show you that being younger or having grown up with access to technology does not guarantee the ability to integrate it meaningfully. Although it's true that this latest generation of students have been raised in the digital era, they still need the experience and critical thinking skills to implement it effectively. As for the seasoned teacher, sometimes experience can get in the way and create a fixed mindset when it comes to change or enhancement of lessons via digital tools.

Fear of Change

In some cases fear of the unknown also gets in the way. Over my nearly two decades of work in education, I regularly encountered teachers who "just didn't get technology" or "weren't very tech-savvy." It's now more than 16 years into the 21st century, yet we still let ourselves fall back on excuses that technology in some ways is beyond us. Never mind that nearly every one of those non-tech-savvy teachers can quickly pull up Pinterest on their phone or create a high-quality graphic organizer on their computer.

The excuse of not being tech-savvy implies that they don't have to even try to change. It also provides them with a safety blanket that discourages them to take risks with technology in their classroom. If they don't' understand it, why would they let their students try it? That same fear is exponentially increased when they feel like they have to "give up control" of the classroom.

Rather than actually thinking through the advantages of having the students engaged deeply in a project, the mind of a technophobe begins to create a multitude of false scenarios. "They could get off-task" or "What if I don't know what they are doing or how to answer their questions?" These are common fear-based questions that prevent any real progress. Although they are also valid concerns, asking the question and not attempting a change, even if it is for the betterment of student learning, in some ways creates a bigger failure. Playing it safe isn't always the correct choice. When it comes to engaging your students in learning by leveraging digital tools provided in a mobile device initiative, it's worth the risk.

You might find that it's not all that bad.

CHAPTER 2

TOP 10 THINGS NOT TO DO

As I mentioned in the introduction, our district committed a couple of cardinal sins when instituting a new initiative. We cut back teachers' extra planning time and reduced the amount of support positions on campuses. These were short-sighted changes made in an attempt to save budget dollars, but they were detrimental to the advancement of the staff's learning with these new devices.

Although we would eventually overcome those mistakes and reinstitute the Educational Technology position as well as adding in an additional planning period, we still made plenty of other mistakes when it came to training staff in a 1:1 environment. The classroom teacher often felt the force of some of those mistakes, but in some cases, they added to the list through their own errors and false assumptions. It is from those errors that this top ten list has been generated. So, when embarking down the journey of mobile learning in your classroom, be sure to remember the mistakes described in this chapter. Although you'll still make oversights and false assumptions of your own, I'm hoping this list provides you with an idea of what to avoid.

1. Do *Not* Forget to Model

Students mimic much of what they see. They also appreciate it when their teachers are learning alongside them. Recently I visited a first grade class where students were learning an app that I had never heard of. The teacher wanted me to guide the lesson, so I began by admitting that I knew nothing about the app and I would love it if some students could explain how to use it and the purpose behind using it for the lesson.

The students couldn't wait to share their knowledge and whenever I asked them how something worked, they were overly eager to share not only with me but also with the class. The teacher walked away from this feeling confident that she also didn't need to know every part of the app or tool and the kids walked away feeling like proud of their knowledge while also learning some much needed trouble-shooting skills for later in life.

Although that works with younger students, older students may see asking for their help as a sign of weakness if respect and rapport aren't established beforehand. I've found that even when doing guest lessons with high school students, if I ask questions and model effective technology use, they are not only more engaged, but also more apt to comply.

If you are teaching a classroom full of mobile devices, don't forget to also use your own mobile device to demonstrate learning. Students can sense the hypocrisy when you ask them to do something with a digital tool that you yourself will not do. "OK, class, I want you to create this collaborative document in Google Docs. When you are finished, download it as a Word doc and email it to me, because I don't like using Google Docs."

Reading between the lines, this behavior essentially says ... "Do as I say, not as I do." Instead, tell the students that you have always been a Microsoft Word user, but you see the advantages to collaborating on a Google Doc, so you are going to take a risk and use it with them. This not only models risk-taking, it empowers the students in the room as they move from learner to teacher. This learning atmosphere is what we need to strive for.

2. Do *Not* Try to Control Everything

In Book 3, I told a story (http://mrhook.it/2eyes) about what happened when we decided to open up YouTube to students in our district. We had been polling the staff and students for months leading up to that decision, and we finally felt we had reached the threshold where a majority (about 75%) of staff felt that allowing students access to this service could help them with their learning and teaching.

The staff not in favor of access were concerned that students would be distracted by the non-educational videos on YouTube (of which there are many, especially about cats doing silly things). One teacher in particular voiced his concerns with me in an email. He wanted to be able to sit at his desk and see everything that every student was viewing on their devices, all on his own screen. He believed that this kind of monitoring would make him more comfortable as a teacher.

My response to him was that there was in fact already an app for this. It is called the "2eyes 2feet" app. The way it works is you as a teacher must stand up from your desk and walk around the room to actively monitor. It works really well when your role as teacher shifts from that of a lecturer of information to that of a facilitator of learning (more on that in a minute). Now, I was telling him this somewhat in jest, but also to make him aware that effective learning for students does mean the teacher must give up some level of control. Just as

Figure 2.1 My mockup of the 2eyes, 2feet app

you can't control everything they are doing or thinking, you don't want to create an environment where all they do is mimic what you do with little retention.

Ask them questions. Encourage them to solve problems where even you might not know the answer. Not only will they be more engaged (and less likely to get off task), but you'd be surprised at what they might learn.

3. Do *Not* Expect Students to Know Everything

Sure they can play Angry Birds and check Facebook, but can they create, edit and send a Pages doc? Kids may have the advantage, as digital natives, of being able to pick up technology much faster than adults, but don't assume they know *when* and *why* to use it, even if they know *how*.

Our students have been raised in a world with touchscreens and instant access to the world of knowledge on the web. I was raised in a world of Commodore 64 and instant access to the world of encyclopedias from Funk & Wagnalls. Despite those generational differences, I don't assume kids will know what to do with technology when we hand it to them. Some very basic skills are lacking, such as organization of their digital work, prioritizing work flow, and even keeping track of a daily calendar.

After our first couple of years of 1:1, we noticed that students were lacking certain base-level skills that were never really covered in class. We began to dedicate the first few days of each school year to some level of student orientation. What we have found is the more time dedicated to this early on (especially with sixth and ninth graders), the more successful students would be down the road. We even created a site for students (made by our Educational Technologist extraordinaire Lisa Johnson) where they could learn what to do step by step. (Student orientation site available here: http://mrhook. it/student1)

Regardless of what we might think of our students' abilities, they don't know everything when it comes to technology.

4. Do *Not* Be Afraid if They Know Something You Don't

While they might not know everything about technology, there may be times when they do know something you do not. Children have the benefit of three things that adults don't have:

1. time,

2. lack of adult responsibility, and

3. lack of fear of trying something new.

You could argue that some adults don't have those same conflicts, but generally we are so busy trying to manage our jobs and our lives outside of work that we don't make time to explore or try new things. With mobile technology, students are adept at learning how these work in a very quick way.

When I was working with a group of fourth grade students recently, I saw many of them creating their own Kahoot! quizzes (https://getkahoot.com). I had mainly only seen teachers make these, but this particular teacher was very comfortable with letting the students have some control of their own learning. She had them creating the quizzes to reinforce their own understanding. As I watched the students work, I tried to resist the temptation to show them how to do something. I sat back and watched as many of the kids did things even I hadn't considered trying.

One of the students complained that he wanted to be able to crop a picture in the quiz he was creating. Before I could even think of a solution, another student shared with him how she could crop in her camera roll before inserting it into the quiz. Although this seems like a small detail, it shows you how creatively students' minds can work if we just give them a little room to demonstrate their learning.

5. Do *Not* Keep Your Successes (and Failures) to Yourself

The teaching profession prescribes *collaboration,* but it doesn't always embody the true meaning of it. The word collaboration comes from a root meaning "co-labor" or working together. In teaching, that might mean planning together or going to a training together, but in actuality that is more cooperating than collaborating.

When I was a teacher, I worked with many teams that were cooperating on lessons more than actually working on them together. If a teacher ever came up with a unique or clever idea that went against the norm, it didn't really matter because everyone just closed their doors and carried on. Taking a risk and either succeeding or failing only really matters for those kids in your class in that closed-door environment.

The truth is, sharing those successes and failures not only can help you grow as a teacher professionally, it also can increase the sense of collaboration among team members. Here are two scenarios:

Scenario 1. Ms. Smith is thinking of trying a new technique to solve math equations using a graphic calculator app like Desmos (https://www.desmos.com) on the students' mobile devices. She has the students download and test the app, then she has them use it during assessments. As it turns out, the kids actually do a much better job understanding algebra when they use the app instead of their graphing calculators. Although she's proud of herself and her students for the work they have done with this new app, no one else even knows what she is trying because she elects to keep this to herself.

As a result of her unwillingness to share, the rest of the math department continues using more standard methods to try and teach these complex concepts. In turn, their students begin to struggle or remain flat in terms of their exam work. The teachers end up despising Ms. Smith because her students' scores are higher and she has never shared why they were better. The whole team ends up fired. (OK, so that last bit was a little harsh. …)

Scenario 2. Ms. Smith starts out her day by sharing this new Desmos app with other teachers on her team. She tells them that she is willing to pilot out this new experience to see how the students will respond to it. An overwhelming number of students are excited to try and learn with this new tools. Other teachers, already aware of what she is doing, ask her to share her discoveries and the logistics of using this app. She gladly walks them through it and shares with them some tips to avoid.

As a result of her willingness to share, the entire team's group of students improves in understanding and in test scores. The entire team is recognized for their innovative work and risk-taking as well as their collaborative efforts to the benefit of their students.

Although these scenarios may seem a little far-fetched, the truth of the matter is that, for whatever reason, some teachers don't feel comfortable sharing. Take baby steps when it comes to sharing and collaboration among peers.

6. Do *Not* Feel as if You're Alone

Teaching, by its nature, is a position that tends to drift toward isolation. Think about all the other jobs in the world. Lawyers, doctors, engineers—all of these work collaboratively to solve problems and to consistently grow. The model for education and the role of the teacher for decades has been not only a "sage on the stage," but also someone who closes their door when the bell rings.

Embarking on the mobile learning path can be a scary predicament even for the most tech-savvy of teachers. When implementing something new with technology, some teachers may feel that they are alone and that others might not support the risk. Others may feel that they may be judged by their peers if they try something new and innovative that their colleagues aren't willing to try. Whatever the reason, know that there are thousands of other teachers like you. The good news is that social media can now help knock down some of those virtual doors for the teacher willing to reach out and share.

Some of the best professional development I have ever received was over social media. Whether it was a conversation of ideas during a Twitter chat or an amazing Pinterest board full of integration ideas, social media not only provides a wealth of resources, but it can also support a teacher.

7. Do *Not* Fall in Love with One Particular App

In the ever-changing world of technology and apps, it's easy to fall in love with a certain app that does a specific thing just the way you want it done. But think of the paradox of that last sentence. If the world of technology is ever-changing, there is some inherent risk in having a particular app as a "digital crutch." That doesn't mean we should necessarily be switching to the latest new thing every few weeks, either. But as teachers, we need to be sure not to get too complacent in the world of apps and programs. That complacency could limit some possibly transformational learning that might take place if our students had some other choices to demonstrate their learning (more on this in Chapter 5).

This doesn't mean that you need to completely overhaul your project or unit from the year before in the name of trying something new, either. Let's say you are teaching a unit that culminates in the students making a movie trailer in an app like iMovie. Although I love the ease with which the movie trailer feature in that app works, it also limits some of what the students can showcase. Rather than toss it and start all over, the next time you have a unit that requires some sort of student showcase of work, let the students choose from a menu of apps. Or better, yet, have them try some new app or program you haven't seen before. You might be amazed at what they come up with.

8. Do *Not* Neglect Parent Communication

Parent communication is important in any classroom, whether it be one that is digitally enhanced with mobile devices or not. In the mobile learning environment though, you are now afforded some new ways to communicate and new channels with which to do so. Social media can be a great ally in the world of parent communication and many classroom teachers are now figuring out ways to engage parents with Facebook pages, Instagram feeds, and Twitter accounts.

Figure 2.2 My daughter's new light-up shirt being shared on her teacher's Instagram feed.

My daughter's first grade teacher regularly uses Instagram to post snapshots of learning almost every day (Figure 2.2). As a parent, when I pick my child up and ask the typical question "What did you do in school today?" I'm better prepared to respond to the typical dreaded answer of "nothing." I now have a glimpse into the classroom that I didn't have before.

Taking this a step further, as we'll hear in the interview with Cathy Yenca in the next chapter, bypassing the teacher-parent communication piece and having students take some level of ownership in sharing information with Mom and Dad can be powerful. Having a class "documentarian" to take a photo or post a tweet every day is a good first step to empowering students on the communication front. Even beyond this, I've visited kindergarten teachers in our district who have their students email completed projects or important work to their parents straight from their devices. Students in those classrooms feel the pride of instantly sharing their work via this digital medium. They are also laying the groundwork for future communication methods they will experience in school and life as they grow older.

9. Do *Not* Assume Traditional Teaching Will Be Best for Learning

There is a time and a place for lectures, but as I said in Chapter 1, we need to shift where information is flowing to or from. With ubiquitous access via some sort of mobile device, this shift begins to take on urgency and necessity. This can be harder in the core curriculum areas where there is a traditional scope and sequence followed by a traditional lesson plan. As a teacher trying to make the change to a more student-focused, problem-based approach, it's sometimes best to start on the edges of curriculum, particularly those that are not part of the core four areas.

One of the best examples of this that I've seen recently was led by a member of my Ed Tech team, Richard Lombardo (@rich_lombardo). Rich supports one of our middle school campuses where we've always had a hard time figuring out how to best introduce and integrate the idea of digital citizenship into the regular school day. We've used resources like Common Sense Media (http://www.commonsense.org) in the past to direct, teach, and ask probing questions, but the students rarely internalized that learning.

Rich decided, with tremendous support from campus leadership (always key), to take a risk and challenge the entire campus of 1,000 students to turn the learning of digital citizenship into a single project-based day. (Check out Rich's blog post about the process here: http://mrhook.it/pbl.) The campus cleared the bell schedule and blocked off an entire day dedicated to this new way of learning. Students formed teams to answer essential questions by planning, designing, shooting, and editing a public service announcement around an important topic related to digital wellness. The entire day was a great success. Students were very engaged in the topic and came away learning more than they would have in a traditional teacher-led lecture. As a result of this risk and success, the school is now considering using "PBL days" for other subject areas like writing and science, something that wouldn't have happened if they had stuck with the status quo in terms of pedagogy.

10. Do *Not* Try to Change Everything Overnight

Teaching is hard. With pressures of test scores, disengaged students, increased parental demands, and a lack of support and training, throwing mobile devices into the mix may seem like the proverbial last straw that broke the teacher's back.

It doesn't have to be.

Realize that human beings are limited in the amount of change they can handle in a given time period. Expecting to completely transform all your lessons and teaching style overnight is unrealistic and sets you up for failure (more on this in Chapter 6).

Instead, identify one or two projects each semester that you could transform with these mobile learning tools. Find a formative assessment tool (Chapter 7) that you can easily introduce and use to get student feedback. Give a little bit of control to the students in your classroom, and ask them to have some say in what the outcome of their learning should be. Making these slight adjustments over time will not only allow you to keep your sanity—it will give you the opportunity to see the value and benefit of having mobile learning in the classroom.

CHAPTER 3

INTERVIEW WITH CATHY YENCA

Part of the joy of doing this book series is getting to interview amazing educators and leaders from all over the world. Each interview for each book has been specific to the focus of the book. I interviewed a principal for the principal book, a district administrator for the district leader book, and so on. Each of those interview subjects holds a special place in my heart, because they greatly influenced much of my own learning.

Cathy Yenca

That said, this might be one of my favorite interviews ever. Cathy Yenca (@mathycathy) is someone I had the good fortune to meet when I hired her husband Tim (@mryenca) as our Mobile Integration Specialist in 2012. He mentioned to me during the interview process that his wife was a phenomenal math teacher who loved to integrate technology in her classroom and wasn't afraid to try something new. She would later interview and gain a position in our district as a middle school math teacher—and the rest, as they say, is history. The following year, Cathy, myself, and Lisa Johnson (whom I've mentioned in just about every book in the series) became a rare triumvirate when all three of us were accepted into the Apple Distinguished Educator program from the same school district.

I've interviewed people from all over the world, but sometimes the most talented people are right in your own backyard. And so, I present my interview with an amazing and inspiring teacher who has truly lived up to her phenomenal status. As with all the interviews, the link at the end will take you to the actual interview captured in video format.

Carl Hooker (CH): Cathy, why don't we start with where this all began? Tell me your origin story and how you got into education.

Cathy Yenca (CY): Sure! So at the moment I teach middle school math to eighth graders, seventh graders, sixth graders, and, this year, even a fifth grader. I teach Algebra 1 PreAP Math.

CH: A fifth grader?!

CY: Yes, he's so cute, because he walks in with a little suitcase because he commutes from his campus next door.

I'm loving middle school. We are in year 4 of 1:1 iPads for me. It's been a real pleasure, and I would not go back. I've been in Austin for about 4 years. Thanks to Carl, our entire family uprooted and moved from Eastern Pennsylvania to Austin. No regrets, as it's really been a fun ride.

That's sort of the present. If I go back to the beginning, it's hilarious—because I did not want to be a teacher.

CH: Hmmm. …

CY: Yeah, it's hilarious because I went to college as an undecided major. I knew I was good at school, but I really didn't know what I wanted to do with that. I guess the truth of the matter is that teaching really found me.

When I went to college, I just remember being in this math class. I knew I wanted to take something with math. This one course I took—I remember there were computer science majors in there that were really struggling and freaking out with the content. I remember taking them under my wing into this empty classroom and trying to teach them how to do proofs outside of class. Really just trying to rescue these guys, because they had no idea what was going on, and I remembered that I really liked the feeling of helping someone else understand math.

Later I would work summers in the Upward Bound program—which was really life-changing for me, working with those at-risk high school kids. To live with them in the dorms and be sort of a camp counselor, but also to help them, since they had class all day and I would tutor them in the evenings. I don't know, I guess [teaching] just sort of found me at the end.

CH: Besides being a great math teacher, you also integrate quite a bit of technology in your classroom. What was your first recollection of technology in school, as a teacher or as a student?

CY: My first handheld device was some sort of TI graphing calculator. When I was in high school I remember using the early models of that. My earliest memory of integrating technology as a teacher was when I would create a PowerPoint presentation and route it through the television. We used to have this thing called "Channel One TV"—I don't know if you remember that.

CH: I remember that!

CY: Yeah, in Pennsylvania, every classroom had this TV in it for Channel One News, so I figured a way to rig a PowerPoint (since we didn't have data projectors then). I rigged PowerPoint to this little old TV. It was so awesome because

I didn't have to turn my back to the students. I didn't have that annoying dry erase marker smear on my hand from using the overhead.

CH: I remember that too! I'd always come home with purple on my hand.

CY: Plus, I could put clip art in there. And I could put students' names in the word problems. That was really huge.

CH: That is awesome, great examples of both.

Flash-forward and think about the juxtaposition of that. Now you have every single student walking in with an iPad. They've had them for several years. So what's one thing you love to do when it comes to mobile devices? Because that's a much different experience than projecting a PowerPoint on a television.

CY: Definitely! Lately it's anything that I can put into a Desmos activity (http://desmos.com), because it's been my thing lately. Instead of me telling the kids something—which would be really easy to do—I'm trying to design an experience for them that's really visual and interactive. Something that by the end of it they are telling me that thing, that would have been so easy for me to just give to them. It's like what textbooks do where they have this "key concept" box. We sometimes start there as a resource, but then taking that key concept box and then thinking as a teacher, "How can I design an experience for my kids?"

CH: So if you look back to your early teaching, do you think your style of teaching has shifted at all the style of teaching you are doing? It sounds like your early experiences were more teacher-directed, whereas now they are a bit more student-centered. Is that accurate?

CY: Yes! I would say definitely when it comes to the technology integration piece. You could make kind of a discovery worksheet back in the day. You could guide them through some investigation where they were doing something on a calculator and it guided them to an experience. But I definitely didn't use technology for anything student-centered. That was selfish. Knowing all my notes so I wouldn't have to write them again. Help with management since my back wasn't to the kids any more. But it really wasn't for them that I did those things, it was more for me.

CH: You inspire a lot of teachers. You publish on your blog (http://mathycathy. com) and put stuff on TeachersPayTeachers (http://teacherspayteachers.com) as well as being a Nearpod PioNear. So where do you go for inspiration?

CY: A very simple hashtag. It's called the #mtbos hashtag on Twitter. It stands for "Math Twitter Blog-o-sphere." It is the real deal. It's amazing. It's a community that really happened organically online through Twitter and through blogging. Some people are more active on Twitter but maybe they don't blog that often, and some are the other way around. I had an opportunity to meet many people in real life from the Math Twitter Blog-o-sphere when I went to Nashville for an NCTM conference (http://www.nctm.org) a couple of months ago.

It was just so cool to see so many people that push me and inspire me in person after respecting their work and really collaborating and tweaking each other's ideas across miles. Someone that I've never met might make a resource. They share it. I tweak it and share it back. They tweak it back and we're really having a literal global PLN. We are sharpening each other daily.

CH: So to follow up on that—not every teacher naturally starts sharing everything they are doing. You didn't just step into a classroom and launch MathyCathy.com. So for the teacher just getting started with sharing, what advice would you have for them to get started sharing their work?

CY: For me, it's kind of personal. I don't have a general story, but for me, the move to Austin in 2012 really sparked it. We moved across the country to Austin to intentionally become part of a 1:1 iPad initiative. That was a milestone. It was a mark on the professional timeline of my career where I began to say "I have a very specific purpose to share what I am doing." I'm doing something that's brand new. It's pioneering. I don't really have a resource to help me do this, so I'm just going to chart my journey hoping that it will be helpful to other people that jump on board. For me that was the impetus to want to share.

I think you have to have a personality that's willing to put yourself out there and also to take constructive criticism. There's a lot of folks out there that are smarter and more creative and have more experience. Instead of viewing that as a negative, I say "I can really tap into this person's expertise, and thank you for making me better."

I guess the words "growth mindset" would be appropriate here. If you have a growth mindset going into your sharing of whatever you are doing, no matter how big or small, put yourself out there and be willing to grow when folks have feedback. I think that's where I would start.

CH: That's kind of the idea behind this book series. It's about mindset, reflection, and taking risks. So speaking of taking risks—have you ever tried something that you thought would be great, but it then completely failed? What was it, and how did you recover from it?

CY: Sometimes I design something, and maybe the furniture or seating arrangement doesn't work. I had this idea where I pictured this interactive activity where kids are talking and interacting and collaborating and justifying. All these great things you want to have happen in a math class. Then all of a sudden they are just sort of clicking through and sitting there.

I'm thinking, "This is really awkward. This is not what I envisioned at all." Taking those moments and pausing, asking questions, getting the kids to talk a little bit and interjecting. Getting them to stop for five seconds and have them turn and talk to someone for five seconds, then ask the question again. It's having that sense to know when things aren't going the way you thought they'd look like and try something different. It's that with-it-ness that comes with good teaching and thinking you may have designed a great resource, but this is not what it looks like.

CH: Design is the first part, but then the delivery and accepting it is a whole other part. Getting them to interact is tricky. Speaking of interaction, I hear this a lot, and it's actually one of the chapters of this book in terms of dealing with classroom management. You mentioned that sometimes it just comes down to good teaching. Do you have any tips out there? How do you handle classroom management now that every student has a mobile device? Are there tips that you can share for the fearful teacher who might not want to deal with these devices from a classroom management perspective?

CY: You have to have a plan, because kids are eventually going to be off task. Even in the most engaging lesson, they'll find a way sometimes. In my case, math class might not be the first priority for these adolescent and pre-adolescent kids. I get that.

My goal is to make a lesson that is so engaging that they won't really have the desire to not do what we are doing. I try to keep that in mind. What would the kids be doing at every moment of this experience? What does that look like? Engaging and designing good lessons is the best way to be proactive.

When the kids do falter—and you know, we're are all humans, so that's going to happen—have a plan in place. The other day, I felt so bad when I saw this screen shot from a student. One of my kiddos was definitely off-task. We were not using iPads at that moment, and you could tell he was doing something, so I told him to take a screenshot, email it to me and someone at home, and if it's not in my inbox in the next five minutes, we're going out to the hallway to have a conversation.

Well, then it shows up in my inbox and I realize he was writing a poem.

CH: Oh no!

CY: You know what I mean? And it was a great poem!

CH: But that's not math. *(laughs)*

CY: *(laughs)* Yes, that's not math. I like to write poems too but not when I'm teaching kids math. It made me feel bad because he was doing something academic but it wasn't in my subject area. But that whole plan about taking a screenshot and then being mortified because now Mom and Dad know about it. I usually follow up with another email explaining to Mom and Dad what the screen shot was all about. Little Johnny was writing a poem during math class when he should have really been focusing on the math.

CH: So sad.

CY: *(laughing)* I know!

CH: A great story. I like the idea of taking a screenshot and sending it home to Mom. The students have some sort of action in this consequence.

CY: Usually that's enough. And when that happens once or twice, the rest of the kids realize it and fall in line. There are so many tools out there now where you can monitor what the kids are doing minute-to-minute. That real-time feedback is so valuable for teaching. If you give them an opportunity where they should really be doing something every second and holding them accountable by you looking at it and everyone looking at it, you are not going to have that happen as much.

CH: Engagement is a big part of that. So for a reluctant teacher—like one that understands the management part, but doesn't know where to get started on learning with mobile devices—is there an app or a tool that you would suggest that would be a lay-up or easy win for a teacher just getting started?

CY: In general, I would say that any tool that fosters the whole formative assessment piece. Whatever that looks like. Making student thinking visible or doing something that has every student involved.

A real simple one that I can think of is Socrative (www.socrative.com). You can ask a kid a question verbally and ask a question on the fly. Especially those moments where you ask a question, but none of the students are engaging, even when you know that at least half of them know the answer to the question.

CH: Yes....

CY: Just launching a quick question. "I need more information from you. Submit your answers, and it can be anonymous, and you have the answers right in front of you." I think any tool that makes the kids' thinking visible and informs instruction and you can show them that feedback. It's pretty painful sometimes. Formative assessment. People always have all these great things to say about it. Its impact on teaching and learning. Almost like, if everything else is terrible and you do formative assessment, the effect size is huge. There is so much research that backs that up.

But no one ever really talks about how painful that can be for the teacher that just thought they taught a great lesson and then you get that information from the kids [that counters that thought]. It's almost like there is this parallel universe that's happening all the time, and you didn't know it.

CH: *(laughs)*

CY: It's like when you discover Twitter and didn't realize all that was there. With formative assessment, it's like you discover what the kids were really thinking, even though you may have thought the learning and the lesson went well—but their answers are way in left field. You have to be able to bite the bullet and take that as reality and figure out what are your next steps.

I think that piece hurts, but you are motivated by it. Now what are you going to do? You have the power to plan those next steps. I felt so horrible when I first discovered that. I thought they knew the content, but discovered that they didn't. I know there are other ways to do that besides using technology, but honestly I don't think it's ever been so easy and efficient as it is now with some of the great tools that are out there.

CH: There's a whole chapter in this book about formative assessment—but you know, I never thought about the psychology behind it. That's a great point. I know Hattie's research points to the .90 effect size on learning, but you're right it's a slam dunk if you can kind of get over the psychology of discovering what the kids actually learned and retained.

CY: Yes! *(laughs)*

CH: So time to change it up and go a little "James Lipton" style here. Just tell me the first thing that pops into your head.

CY: OK. *(laughs)*

CH: I'm going to put on my British accent for this. No, not really. So, let's start with this—what's your favorite word?

CY: "Parapluie"—it's French for umbrella. *(laughs)*

CH: Um … OK. I wasn't ready for that one … um … interesting.

CY: See! I love that made your rapid fire completely fall apart! Awesome! I'm so proud of myself!

CH: *(laughs)* On my first question! What's your least favorite word? Although I'm afraid to ask now.

CY: Puke.

CH: Don't like the sound or what it intends. ...

CY: No.

CH: If you couldn't be a teacher, what would you be?

CY: A singing interior decorator/real estate agent. That would probably be a thing in Austin, wouldn't it?

CH: That would. That's a reality TV show right there!

CY: There you go.

CH: I don't think you are actually very far from that to be honest, but OK. *(Laughs)*

CY: *(Laughs)*

CH: Name something cool that you have in your classroom.

CY: I have this sunburst mirror, but all the sunburst things are warped wooden rulers that were going to be in the trash.

CH: Oh! A little remixing and upcycling there. Nice. What's something that you think needs to be invented?

CY: When I was a little girl, I used to think, why can't they just paint a stripe in the middle of the road and then program cars to follow that stripe so no one gets in an accident anymore? What's ironic about that is that I remember that as early as preschool. Kind of the first idea of a driverless car. Maybe that's not a good example, because I think that's kind of already in the works, huh?

CH: An autonomous car following the magnetic strip? You were kind of onto something there. Ok, so you mentioned you were a singer, so when was the last time you sang?

CY: Honestly, it was in the car this morning in the parking lot.

CH: And the song was?

CY: It's that new song "Piece by Piece" by Kelly Clarkson. She doesn't know we sang a duet this morning, but it was really good.

CH: What motto or expression do you like to live by?

CY: "A smile confuses an approaching frown."

CH: Powerful! Any final advice for a teacher that's trying to get out there with mobile learning and sharing? Any last tips?

CY: Give yourself grace—but not so much that it paralyzes you from trying things and being the self-motivated, independent learner that you want your students to be. How about that?

CH: That is perfect! Thank you so much for taking the time to be a part of this, and we look forward to seeing all the work you share at your website (http://mathycathy.com) and on Twitter (@mathycathy).

CY: Thank you so much, Carl!

To watch this interview in it's entirety, go here: http://mrhook.it/mathycathy

CHAPTER 4

MANAGING THE CLASSROOM WITH ENGAGEMENT

One thing I have observed about technology is that it is a great amplifier. It can make a good teacher great, and a bad teacher worse. I know that's a very broad generalization, but in visiting hundreds of classrooms with mobile devices, I've gleaned some consistent trends when it comes to classroom management and student behavior.

I vividly remember walking into the classrooms of Westlake High School during the first couple of months of our WIFI (Westlake Initiative For Innovation) pilot. It was common to see kids taking notes on their iPads and surfing the web for research. However, it was also common to see a handful of students in the back of the class tilting their iPad from side-to-side with their tongues sticking out of the corner of their mouths. It was pretty obvious that these kids were playing some sort of racing game rather than paying attention to the lecture.

At that time, the kinds of restrictions we could put on the devices were limited. The iPads could either be turned into kiosks, or be more open to offer exploration and expand creativity by allowing access to the entire app store (with some restriction). A great deal has changed since then, and there are ways to lock down and manage most mobile devices as long as they are under the supervision of the district. Many teachers reading this book are likely dealing with another scenario of students bringing in their own devices (BYOD). In that situation, the ability to control goes out the window. But although that can be a stressful crutch to give up, in some ways it can be freeing. The tips relayed in this chapter are laid out with the assumption that the teacher has no technical way to lock down and manage devices at the classroom level.

Fear of Lack of Control

When I started out as a classroom teacher, I always perceived the need to be in control. I didn't realize until later in my teaching career that if I shared some ownership of the classroom with the students, they not only learned more, their behavior improved.

That said, I only had four computers in the back of my classroom and the occasional laptop cart of white Apple iBooks. Students were supervised for the most part, but there were times when I'd be helping some students and a fellow classmate would accidentally arrive somewhere online where they weren't supposed to be. I couldn't be everywhere at once, and the fact that students had access to this thing called the internet meant I had two choices: run away from the technology, or embrace it.

When students walk into a classroom with mobile devices in hand, teachers are faced with this same choice. In the first year of our 1:1, the teachers who applied to be in the pilot obviously embraced it. However, those who were not a part of the original pilot group elected to avoid the challenges and insisted on having "no technology allowed" signs posted outside their doors. When I asked these teachers about their stance on this, they had a myriad of reasons for not allowing technology, but the majority boiled down to one simple tenet: They were afraid to give up control.

Responses to my question from these teachers included, "Why would I let the kids be distracted from what I'm trying to teach them?" or "How can I hold their attention when they have access to everything at their fingertips?"

That fear of letting go not only limits the possibilities with technology integration, it also places much of the power of learning firmly on the shoulders of the teacher. The student role in this environment is very passive, sitting back and absorbing information as it's presented to them. The teacher's role is one of control, pacing, and very much repetition—not only of information, but also of ways to solve the problems.

2 Eyes, 2 Feet

In 2013, after much research and polling of staff and students, we decided to open up YouTube Safe Search to students. Although there are a lot of mind-numbing videos about squirrels on jet-skis, there is also a large amount of instructional content on there. Want to learn how to use Photoshop? Or maybe the right way to carve a turkey? It's all on YouTube.

Ten minutes after announcing that YouTube would be open for students, I received the following email (Figure 4.1) from a concerned teacher. For the sake of anonymity, I'll refer to him as "Jim."

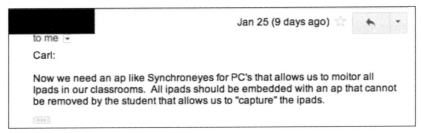

Jan 25 (9 days ago)

to me

Carl:

Now we need an ap like Synchroneyes for PC's that allows us to moitor all
Ipads in our classrooms. All ipads should be embedded with an ap that cannot
be removed by the student that allows us to "capture" the ipads.

Figure 4.1 A teacher's concern over YouTube

Jim's concern here is real. Teachers want to be able to monitor students from
the comfort of their desks and "guarantee" that they are paying attention
during the lecture or working on what they should be. Although there are
applications that can do this now, at the time the choices were fairly limited.
Technology can help us solve problems, such as by forcing students to focus on
the lecture at hand, but it doesn't fix the larger problem: why the students are
distracted in the first place. It's like asking someone to quit smoking by taking
away the cigarette but not addressing the habit or reasoning behind their need
to smoke.

One of the other issues with the viewing and monitoring of student devices
from a teacher's desk is that proximity and interaction with the actual students
ceases to exist in some ways. Although this makes life easier for the teacher, it's
not helping the students learn how to stay focused and engaged. In Jim's case,
learning wasn't the primary objective—he wanted to be able to control them.

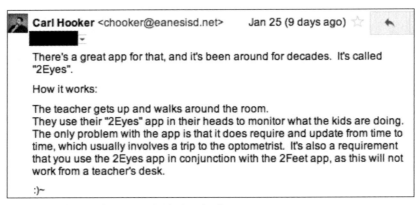

Carl Hooker <chooker@eanesisd.net>   Jan 25 (9 days ago)

There's a great app for that, and it's been around for decades. It's called
"2Eyes".

How it works:

The teacher gets up and walks around the room.
They use their "2Eyes" app in their heads to monitor what the kids are doing.
The only problem with the app is that it does require and update from time to
time, which usually involves a trip to the optometrist. It's also a requirement
that you use the 2Eyes app in conjunction with the 2Feet app, as this will not
work from a teacher's desk.

:)~

Figure 4.2 My email response to the teacher's concern

Figure 4.2 shows my response to Jim. I made sure to include the all-important smiley face, so he knew I was being somewhat tongue-in-cheek, but I was also sincere in asking him to think about shifting the pedagogical practice he was employing. I later regretted not adding the statement that you can also use your "iMouth" to enforce restrictions.

I later went to Jim's class and had a conversation about the issues and concerns he was facing. Our talk quickly transitioned from placing the blame on the students to looking internally at his own pedagogical philosophy. Jim felt he had been "successful" with the lecture method for many years because students were doing well on their tests. When I asked him if his students learned from him, he said that he assumed they did, because their test scores were good. Our educational system is set up to reward that kind of thinking and outcome, so in some ways, Jim felt that he had done his job as a teacher because of those scores.

Earning Student Engagement

Jim's need to control his students, and his belief that they were doing fine because of their test scores, is nothing new. These beliefs are ingrained in education and, to some extent, taught through our university systems. In 2013, I was giving a guest lecture to a group of preservice teachers at a local university. I was discussing the various forms of technology and social media tools available to them and asking them how they used technology. I noticed that although almost all of them had some sort of laptop or device out, only half were paying attention to what I was saying.

I immediately decided to use my 2 Eyes, 2 Feet app and moved from the stage to the back of the classroom while never breaking from my lecture, as I was curious what they were engaged with. Some, I found, were researching me and my background. Some were looking for tools and strategies for things I was discussing with them. They were engaged with what I was saying, but also digging deeper into the points I was raising.

Although that made me feel better, I also noticed about half the students were totally engaged in other things—looking up floral patterns on Pinterest, reading up on their favorite reality television star, or chatting with a friend somewhere else in the world. Rather than expressing my frustration, I asked them about what they were doing. I wasn't trying to embarrass them, but instead to learn why they weren't engaged in the conversation we were having.

It turned out that many felt that although I did ask them to think and discuss at times, primarily what I was doing was lecturing "at" them. They were paying attention to about half of what I was saying, and spending the rest of their attention on other items that interested them.

This lead to a great whole-class discussion about what environments these soon-to-be teachers would be walking into, and how they could earn their students' full attention. Through our discussions that day, the group came to the conclusion that student attention was nice, but more importantly, we wanted the students to be engaged with learning, not just with what the teacher was saying.

In a lecture format, creating engagement and attention lies completely on the shoulders of the teacher. Keeping the students engaged means a lot of high-quality storytelling, visuals, and mixing in the occasional discussion time. This requires a great deal from a teacher ahead of time and during the lesson in order to ensure engagement. You can pretty much assume that students are getting the exact same experience, since it's funneled through you as a teacher—but this means that there isn't any real level of differentiation or opportunity for questions and experiences.

You can see the inherent issues that might arise from bringing technology and devices into this environment. Now the student has an opportunity to engage in a deeper learning experience—or be completely distracted. It all depends on the student's own level of responsibility.

Centering Learning around the Student

In looking at the examples I've just given, it becomes more and more obvious that in order to truly capture students' attention and engage them, the learning must be centered around them. There is a big difference between saying that and actually doing that, and it's not something that happens overnight. And, as we've seen up to this point, the fear of losing control and the need to deliver all content to the students can get in the way of it happening at all.

The reason project- and inquiry-based learning models work so well is that they shift the heavy lifting of learning from the shoulders of the teacher to the brains of the students. Making that shift doesn't happen overnight, but it can be done with some simple first steps. One of those first steps that I've seen work well is letting students make some choices as to how they will demonstrate their learning.

I once visited a third grade class that was doing a unit on celestial bodies in our solar system. The teacher had planned to give them some time to research their object of choice and then asked them to create a presentation using the Keynote app on their iPads. When I asked her why she chose that, she said it was a program she had used before and felt most comfortable helping them with it if they ran into any issues. I then asked the students if there were other programs that they could use to demonstrate their learning. They mentioned a few other apps, like iMovie and Explain Everything. The teacher, hesitating only briefly, then asked the students which apps they preferred. Students listed several different choices that they felt comfortable using.

In a couple of cases, the students mentioned apps that the teacher wasn't aware of. Rather than turn them down because of her own discomfort, she instead asked them to come up and give a brief demonstration of the app and how they would be using it. She then turned and looked at me and said, "Wow, that wasn't so bad. In fact, it was actually kind of cool!"

She had created a safe environment and encouraged the students to try something new. She realized that by making it a lesson around a certain app or a lesson that followed specific directions, she wasn't making it about the learning. One other thing that became obvious throughout that and subsequent lessons was that the devices and technology were almost invisible during the process. The teacher in a fully integrated classroom wouldn't tell the students, "All right, class—let's take out our iPads and do an iPad lesson about iPads." Instead it was all about the learning objective and the students using their devices to demonstrate their understanding of what they had learned.

Expectations and Ground Rules

Although ideally the focus isn't on the device, some classroom ground rules should be created and expectations shared around student behavior when using mobile devices. In the classrooms where this has worked the best, the teacher engages the learners in the process of creating the rules. That way, the students take some level of ownership when the rules are actually posted.

For example, rules and expectations can be created around the following categories:

- Expected use when someone is presenting/speaking

- Expected use when collaborating with peers

- Expected use when doing independent work

- Expected use during transition time or "free time"

- Expectations while interacting online

- Expectations of home use

Each of these have different levels of expectations based on the maturity of the students. Following are some examples I've seen in classrooms that deploy mobile devices into the hands of students on a regular basis.

Elementary

An elementary classroom with mobile devices can be a great place to introduce first-time expectations of use. Having a poster around the room with the class-generated expectations is always a good introductory activity. Similarly, using simple directions like "Apples up" (for students to close their iPads and flip them over) or "Lids closed" is effective for when students need to focus on instructions or when someone (either a teacher or student) is presenting.

Because not all classrooms may have 1:1 devices at the elementary level, having expectations around shared devices also becomes important. In some cases, students may have access to other students' work, so not deleting, modifying, or moving other students' files is important. Luckily, with more devices moving toward cloud backups and shared management, this is becoming less of an issue. When students are using the devices during an unmonitored center, it's important that students understand what is expected of them and what the consequences are for getting off-task.

One other point I would stress at an early stage is the way that students communicate online with each other. Although elementary students aren't old enough to be interacting on social media (most have a 13+ rule), laying the groundwork here will lead to much more successful decisions and greater awareness of being positive digital citizens later in life. See the following lesson as an example of how to set this up and model and discuss how students should behave online.

EXAMPLE LESSON

Early Digital Citizenship Activity: Appropriate online behavior

Resources Needed: Mobile devices, access to the internet

Concept: Students practice interacting with each other online in a sheltered online environment.

Lesson: Using the website http://todaysmeet.com, create a room where students will interact. Start by discussing the pros and cons of being anonymous online and what potential problems could result. Ask students to post their feelings or thoughts about a discussion that recently took place in class. Have them respond to each other in the online room, and model appropriate online behavior.

Extension: Use a chat room as a backchannel while watching a film or video so that everyone has an opportunity to contribute.

Secondary

In a secondary environment with mobile devices, student behavior can be a much tougher thing to manage. Because students are constantly moving from class to class, the campus needs to have clearly defined expectations and consequences around device use. Having a strong acceptable use policy (or, as we call it, Responsible Use Guideline) is also a great tool to communicate the responsibilities of students in a mobile device environment.

Much as in an elementary classroom, there needs to be some discussion around those categories listed a few sections earlier. Whether they are presenting, working, or in groups, the expectations for device use can adapt to the situation. One of the first issues we encountered with our mobile device initiative was the lack of responsible behavior students showed during transition time. Because there are no adults supervising them between classes, this is generally when students will push the restrictions on the device or discover non-instructional uses for it.

Many students use this time between classes or at lunch to play games or watch YouTube videos that interested them. As no teacher has authority over the students at that moment, teachers often turn the other way while this happens. Many of the discipline cases land on the desks of assistant principals, the educational technologist, or the librarian. Student expectations need to be agreed upon throughout the school and supported by the entire staff. As a classroom teacher, you can support this in your classroom and as you walk the halls. Luckily, most of the 1:1 devices now have some level of built-in monitoring or restriction software, but in a BYOD environment, that wouldn't be the case.

Responsible Use Guidelines and Device Contracts

In the book for district administrators, I outlined some of the ideas behind a responsible use guideline for staff and students. Within those guidelines for students, there should be leveled approaches to appropriate use. An elementary student might not have to deal with cyberbullying; a high school student might not have to learn how to use email appropriately. In some of the more successful classroom environments, teachers or schools have put a student contract in place for a particular device.

In our schools we created an iPad contract (http://mrhook.it/oath) that each student signs during the first day of orientation. Contained within the contract are expectations of use and consequences for inappropriate use. Although the first reaction of a teacher (or parent) encountering inappropriate use might be to take the device away, I would caution teachers and schools against doing this right away. Not only does it not teach the student responsible use, it takes away a learning tool.

You wouldn't take away a student's pencil if he or she was drawing inappropriate pictures. You would address the behavior. The same can be said of technology. Again, those in 1:1 environments have some more advanced tools available to them when it comes to restrictions and monitoring. In our environment, after a few years of wrestling with the right level of restrictions, we turned off access to the public app store. Students can only download apps that have been approved by the staff and that appear in the district app store on the device. Although this does restrict some of the spontaneity and discovery of apps, limiting this on the device reinforces the idea that it is truly an instructional device.

In a BYOD environment, a similar oath should be written with students around expectations when using their own devices. As you won't have the restrictions of a district-owned device, you'll want to brainstorm with students about what would be appropriate and inappropriate. Using the categories listed at the beginning of this chapter would help, but also keep in mind that now they can receive text messages, play any game they want, access all social media, and put their own videos and photos on the device. Each of these brings with it more opportunities to learn about responsible use of their own devices as we prepare our students for the next-generation workplace and for college.

In the coming chapters, I'll show different ways that you can use the classroom environment, instructional strategies, and content to help manage the classroom beyond just a baseline of rules or a student contract.

CHAPTER 5

THE LEARNING ENVIRONMENT

Where do you go when you want to learn or create? I've asked this question to many groups of teachers, students, and leaders. The responses vary from "on my couch with a cup of coffee" to the local coffee shop. I know when it came to writing this book series, I spent a great deal of time at the Strange Brew Coffeehouse typing away with many other writers, artists, and musicians in my own comfy chair or private corner.

When you are thinking of your own responses, ask if any of them involve a classroom. It's kind of scary to think that isn't one of the first places you think about, considering that classrooms are where we want students to learn. Everyone has their own preference, and generally a classroom space is limited by both size and choice of furniture. Both of these limitations make it difficult for students to personalize their preferred physical learning environment.

With the addition of mobile devices, it might make sense that the classroom environment would also become a more mobile space. However, time and time again, when I walk into classrooms there are still desks in rows, and instead of students quietly sitting there reading books or taking notes, they are reading ebooks and taking notes on their devices. In some ways, not much has changed, even with technology added to the mix.

In my classroom at the turn of the century, technology was essentially a bank of computers at the back of the classroom. Students would play games like *Oregon Trail* or *Where in the World Is Carmen San Diego?* for 15 minutes a week, and the teacher could check off a little box indicating that students used technology for learning. I was limited by my space because the machines had to be hard-wired into the classroom wall. That is not the case anymore.

Effective Work Spaces

In 2008, the Gensler group commissioned a study (http://mrhook.it/gensler) to research businesses that had the most effective and innovative workforce. The main objective of the research was to see if there was anything about their work spaces that helped make these businesses more successful. It turned out that these places of business had four work spaces in common. The four spaces were:

1. Focus Space

2. Learning Space

3. Collaborative Space

4. Social Space

Although our classrooms are limited by the four walls that surround them, there are ways we can take advantage of the mobility that students with devices can offer in each of these spaces.

Focus Space

This space is defined as a place to concentrate on an individual project or task. In the workplace, this is generally a desk where you would sit (or stand). In schools, this area is clearly defined by the all-in-one student desk. Although uncomfortable (more on that later in this chapter), desks do provide students with space of their own to focus on individual assignments, lecture, or, more likely, taking tests in isolation.

Learning Space

When a business has to address all its employees or stakeholders, a large meeting room, foyer, or presentation space is often used. There is generally a large presentation screen with audio/visual setup and some sort of voice amplification. In schools these spaces exist both in classrooms (usually marked by the area where the projector is focused) and in a larger assembly space (usually a cafeteria, gymnasium, or some sort of performing arts center). These spaces are used to give general instructions to the entire class or school, and as spaces for students and staff to present information or final products. Much like the focus space, learning spaces exist throughout most schools and in some cases have been overemphasized to the point where teachers become the dreaded "sage on the stage."

Collaborative Space

Space for collaboration is much more than a typical meeting room in the modern business. When I toured the Googleplex in 2013 (see Figure 5.1), there were multiple small rooms built for four or five people. These rooms were surrounded by glass, provided some whiteboard space on the table and wall, and usually had a large LED television for projecting larger ideas.

In contrast to learning and focus spaces, schools tend to struggle making spaces for students to collaborate. There is usually a conference room or teachers' lounge for staff, but students' "collaborative space" is often limited to a few tables in the library. In the classroom, when furniture allows for it, collaborative space can happen almost instantly. Many classrooms from elementary to secondary are shifting toward the concept of seating by tables. This allows instantly for some level of collaboration, but it also creates issues during the dreaded "testing season," as collaboration on tests is called cheating in our world.

Figure 5.1 My visit to the Googleplex

Social Space

Although being social may seem counterintuitive to being productive, the most successful businesses allow for, and in some cases encourage, employees to socialize. In companies like Apple, Facebook, and Google, creating spaces where employees from different departments can co-mingle encourages collaboration and innovation. At Google, employees never go more than 100 feet without access to food and beverages in a "micro-kitchen" that very much resembles that found in a teachers' lounge. It's in these spaces that a person wrestling with a better email solution could encounter a programmer who has an idea for doing it better … and then, Gmail is born. In schools, social space is generally confined to the playground, the cafeteria, or the hallways. Modern businesses have discovered that their employees not only are more innovative, but can actually be more productive when given time and space to socialize.

In our classrooms, we should allow for some of this, too, whether it's during a transition time in elementary classrooms or at a mid-class brain break in secondary classrooms.

Flexibility for a Variety of Tasks

Taking into account the four areas of space in the Gensler study, we know that the typical classroom excels in a couple of areas (focus and learning) but not so much in others (collaborative and social). Much of this is due to pedagogical practices that encourage a single source of information being presented to an assembly line of listeners. Other reasons for this rigidity are the actual capabilities of the furniture in the room.

Unfortunately, as teachers and administrators, we don't all have unlimited funds to outfit our classrooms with the latest and greatest flexible furniture. In one of our "transformative" classrooms, we did raise enough funds to outfit the space with a variety of furniture types. Some of our schools elected to do this with a shared space, while others had teachers apply to have the flexible furniture in their class.

Having teachers apply to have this newer, more mobile furniture in their classroom let us make sure that some thought had been put into how the pedagogy and instructional practice would best use this space. Also, rather than outfit the entire classroom with 22 movable student desks, we used a variety of desks, tables, chairs, and stools that would allow for some personalized preference for each student. Certain students gravitated toward the taller stool and pub-table setup. Others tended toward the Hokki stool (http://vs.de/en/hokki/), which has a rounded bottom so that a student sitting on it needs to engage their core muscles to stay balanced.

Although having movable chairs and wobbly stools may seem like a management nightmare, students quickly adjusted to the new flexible format. While we did have something of a "bumper car" experience during the first week at middle school, students quickly settled into a routine with the new furniture. Not unlike when students begin to use technology, there was a slight uptick of behavior to manage initially while ground rules were laid out.

The advantages of having movable furniture become readily apparent. Students can quickly move into collaborative groups or pairs to work on projects. Teachers begin to experiment with multiple formations of classroom setup and in some scenarios even create a "fish bowl" setup during Socratic seminars. (More on this here: http://mrhook.it/flexible.) Some of the students liked the changes so much that they wrote to the furniture manufacturers to ask for donations, and even presented their findings to the school board one evening. During that board meeting, the students asked the board members to sit in the all-in-one traditional desks while they sat in the new flexible desks. Then they proceeded to do a mock lesson and have the "students" (in this case the board members) create different collaborative formations and arrangements, from partners to large groups to Socratic circles, timing the amount of transition time required for the board members to drag their desks around. The results left quite an impression on our school board, and we now have funds coming in to continue to update our traditional furniture to a more flexible type.

Death of the Student Desk

Speaking of board members—when I present at events around the country, I find myself asking the crowd, "Who has the most comfortable chairs in schools?" Responses usually range from teachers to principals and, eventually, school board members. I always found it somewhat ironic that our school board members, although great supporters of our system, spend only a few hours twice a month in beautiful, plush chairs while our students spend many hours daily in those all-in-one torture devices known as the traditional student desk.

After spending an entire day as a student (http://mrhook.it/s4ad) and sitting in those contraptions, I realized that we need to be thinking past just technology when it comes to updating the learning environment. After my experiment and the students' "collaboration" experiment with the school board, we found some momentum of support from the community to replace the all-in-one chair with something more flexible and mobile. Of course, just changing furniture (much like giving each student a device) does little to change the actual learning environment if instruction is still a traditional, lecture-based model.

As those board members saw, the type of seating and arrangement of furniture can have a great impact on the learning environment when used purposefully. The traditional student desk and the idea of desks in rows exist primarily for custodial purposes rather than learning purposes—it's easier to clean when there are aisles in between desks. This new mobile model allows for optimal learning in a variety of situations in the classroom. Although flexible furniture is still an expensive proposition, teachers in our district have found ways to "hack" their space with a variety of bean bag chairs, pub tables, and yoga balls purchased at garage sales or online. And, as I like to point out, the most flexible learning environment in the world is right outside the walls of the school and costs nothing. So, when all else fails, have class outside!

Using "Dead" Space

Every school building has areas that were designed for architectural purposes rather than learning purposes. I've been in beautiful libraries that look incredible but don't really have the acoustics or sufficient room to be used as an instructional space. Walk up and down the hallways of schools, and you might discover there are spaces where students have carved out a place to learn and collaborate.

These "dead" spaces can be a great way to optimize square footage in a building and to create room for collaboration space for students. When I visited Pershing Elementary School in Berwyn, IL (http://pes.bsd100.org), I was amazed at how well they used dead space. The building was more than 50 years old, but students had found places where they could either focus or collaborate. One such space (Figure 5.2) existed in the stairwell. Rather than waste the space, the school decided to open it up and added some plants and tables to make it more personalized. Because of the openness and exposure to natural light, students would gravitate (and in some cases run) to this space to work.

Figure 5.2 A great use of dead space at Pershing Elementary School in Berwyn, IL.

As a classroom teacher, you might feel limited to keeping the learning inside your classroom. But, be on the lookout for dead spaces like stairwells and hallways as potential areas where student learning and collaboration can take place. You never know—you could turn that old storage closet into a dynamic collaboration space just by removing the door and adding a whiteboard.

Color and Light

One of the final things to consider about a learning environment is the color and light within the room or space. In 2013, we had a teacher ask for permission to repaint her classroom. She had grown tired of what I call the "sanitarium off-white" color that covers the cinder-block walls of many schools built in the past several decades. She was eventually given permission to paint one of the walls an "accent" color. So, over the summer, she and her husband purchased around $50 worth of paint and began painting their accent wall. After they finished, they looked at the rest of the classroom and those three off-white walls staring back at them. Since no one from maintenance was around to help or supervise the project, they took it upon themselves to paint the other three walls a bright orange color. Sometimes it's better to ask for forgiveness than permission.

The result was shocking, in a good way (to see images in full color, visit http://mrhook.it/desk). Walking into the classroom, I instantly felt comfortable. I came back for the first day of class to follow up with the teacher and asked her how parents responded to seeing this new style of classroom. The parents were overwhelmingly positive. One even remarked, "If my classroom looked like this, I might have been more interested in attending." As a result of this teacher's risk-taking, we've now begun to offer a palette of choices for teachers when it comes to wall color. In order to be cost-effective, we don't have every color in the rainbow, but using the latest brain research, we decided on a set of six or eight lighter pastel colors to accent the regular classroom. Slight alterations in paint can be a cost-effective way to enhance the atmosphere of the classroom.

As with wall colors, lighting has always been an afterthought in education. Because fluorescent bulbs take the least amount of maintenance and put out more light with the least amount of energy, schools and districts purchase these as a way of saving money.

Recent research (http://mrhook.it/lighting) has shown that the type of lighting around us can affect our productivity and creativity. The use of indirect or incandescent lighting can help battle the high levels of blue light given off by screens and devices. It also reduces glare and creates a warmer atmosphere for learning.

With updates in lighting technology like the LiFx (www.lifx.com) and Phillips Hue (www2.meethue.com/en-us), not only can you get a longer lasting bulb (these LED bulbs claim a 25-year life span), but you can also control the color of the environment with the click of a button on your smartphone. So even if you are required to keep the institutional off-white color on your walls, you can change the color of the lighting to enhance the learning situation. Imagine the effect of discussing ocean life with your class while the room suddenly starts to become blue.

Taking Pool Breaks

Creating a learning environment that is flexible and adaptable that allows for regular movement can actually help with student retention and learning. One aspect of mobile learning that is often overlooked is the need to take "pool breaks" throughout the day. In the SAMR Swimming Pool analogy (http://mrhook.it/pool) I reference in Chapter 6, I discuss the variety of depths to which you can integrate technology into the classroom with my own spin on Dr. Ruben Puentedura's SAMR model.

That said, having students plugged into devices and screens all day isn't a productive (or healthy) learning environment. Research from Dr. Charles H. Hillman of the University of Illinois (http://mrhook.it/breaks) shows that students' and adults' brains are much more engaged following some sort of movement or activity. Having a short break in the middle of a lengthy period of silence or lecture can re-engage the learner and help with their retention and attention. A learning environment with movable furniture that is adaptable and flexible will help increase movement and opportunities for brain breaks in the classroom.

Here are a few of my favorite brain breaks that I've used for both adults and students. Many more of these can be found by searching the #brainbreak hashtag on Twitter or by searching for "brain breaks" or "improv ideas" on your preferred search engine of choice.

"1, 2, 3"

1. Have students partner up.

2. One student begins counting "1," their partner responds "2," then back "3," then start over.

3. If a pair makes a mistake, have them "celebrate" failure by raising their hands and shouting "Woo hoo!"

4. After 15 or 20 seconds, begin to introduce replacements for numbers with some sort of motion (i.e., clap instead of saying "1," stomp instead of saying "2")

This one is great for getting students up, moving, laughing, and celebrating their mistakes.

Ear Acupressure

1. Stand up straight.

2. Pinch your left ear lobe with your right hand, thumb in front.

3. Cross your left arm over your right and pinch the right ear lobe with your left hand, thumb in front.

4. Gently squeeze both ear lobes at the same time.

5. Place the tip of your tongue on the roof of your mouth just behind your front teeth.

6. Inhale through your nose 15 times.

This is a great one to improve focus but it also is said to help with headaches!

Giant Rochambeau

1. Students find a partner to play Rock-Paper-Scissors.

2. The winning student moves on to face someone else; the losing student becomes their cheerleader.

3. As students win, their cheering section grows until there are only two students left with half the class cheering for one student and the other half cheering for the other.

A great way to promote supporting each other with a touch of competitiveness.

Multitasking Challenge

1. Ask students to stand up.

2. Have them rub their heads while patting their stomachs.

3. After a few seconds, ask them to continue doing that while standing on one leg.

4. Now ask them to continue, but with their eyes closed.

This awakens the brain because of all the movement and is fun to watch as a teacher, especially when students begin to sway from side to side in the room.

These brain breaks are just a few examples of ways to liven up the learning environment and reengage the brain for learning. A teacher who feels pressure to "get through the content" may think that taking a five-minute break in the middle of a lesson will detract from the students' learning. In fact, as research has shown, the opposite might be true. Taking time to increase oxygen flow to the students' brains will open up the neural pathways that help with retention and learning.

Creating structures that focus on the four types of effective spaces in the Gensler study is a great start for teachers looking to change the environment in their classroom. Bringing in furniture that is flexible and adaptable based on the instructional objective can cut back on transition times and create a more collaborative environment. Using dead space both within and outside of the classroom can expand the areas where learning can take place. Adjusting the color and lighting of the learning environment can create a sense of comfort and even encourage more productive learning.

However, all of these adaptations of the traditional learning environment will be moot if the classroom teacher isn't willing to alter their pedagogy to some extent in order to make use of these new flexible environments. In the next chapter, we'll look at how making some small changes to pedagogy can go a long way toward improving the learning experience for students.

CHAPTER 6

SMALL CHANGES AND THE SAMR MODEL

When I first started my current role, I felt as if there were a thousand different things that I needed to do. Besides sorting out all the technology that we had purchased, I also wanted to figure out what subscriptions were being used, what training we were offering, and what the needs of the teachers were. I tried to tackle all of these issues at once and quickly became overwhelmed.

Introducing technology into the hands of students can be overwhelming in much the same way for teachers. Besides sorting out all the apps or programs that can be used, teachers are also balancing new district initiatives, cramming through curriculum, and dealing with assessments, grading, and parents. To tackle all of this at once can become overwhelming, and many teachers are tempted to abandon the latest new thing (in this case, devices) for the things they are most comfortable with.

Changing Habits

The human mind can only handle so much change from routine and habits. During her session at the 122nd annual convention of the American Psychological Association, Wendy Woods stated, "The thoughtful intentional mind is easily derailed and people tend to fall back on habitual behaviors. Forty percent of the time we're not thinking about what we're doing." Wood went on to explain that "habits allow us to focus on other things. ... Willpower is a limited resource, and when it runs out you fall back on habits."

As teachers, we can only expect to change so much of that reaction to what isn't routine. As Wood explains, everyone's will power is limited when it comes to change of habit. That said, we can make small changes in our routine and at first find places where technology "fits in." Eventually, though, using technology at just a substitutive level needs to evolve into a habit so that it can be used for deeper thoughts. That comes with sustained, supported use of mobile devices in the classroom. That also comes with an awareness of what "deeper" learning looks like.

Swimming in the SAMR Pool

Before our own mobile device initiative, I spent a couple of years researching best practices and similar use cases in education. It turned out that 1:1 wasn't a new concept at all. The state of Maine began their Learning Technology Initiative in 2001 (aka "MLTI"—www.maine.gov/doe/mlti/) and had already experienced years of speed bumps and road blocks along their journey. One particular researcher, Dr. Ruben Puentedura (hippasus.com/blog/), had been studying the effects of technology on learning since the late 1980s. When MLTI was launched, he focused his energy and research around this statewide initiative and gathered some great data about what really makes a difference for learning with devices.

Through his research, he developed the SAMR model (http://mrhook.it/samr1). The SAMR model identifies four different levels of student use of: Substitution, Augmentation, Modification, and Redefinition. It was great to see use of technology synthesized in nice, easy-to-grasp levels like those in SAMR. The one drawback of the model that I always saw was that it was designed to look like a ladder, which implied that, as a teacher, you need to have your students climb to the top (Redefinition) to be successful. In reality, it was much different from that. As I began to have a conversation about this with good friend and colleague Greg Garner (http://twitter.com/classroom_tech), he mentioned to me that it was more like a swimming pool than a ladder. I totally bought into his thought process and ran with it, creating my own version of the SAMR model like a swimming pool (Figure 6.1) and writing two blog posts about the idea.

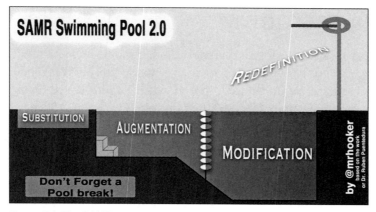

Figure 6.1 The SAMR swimming pool.

The basic concept aligns with SAMR in that the first two levels (Substitution and Augmentation) really fall into the Enhancement level of learning with technology. This is like being in the shallow end of the swimming pool, in that students are somewhat safe from drowning and can still enjoy the water. Technology in the enhancement level is much the same way. Students can enjoy the technology with firm controls and guidance from the teacher, but without going off on their own and "drowning" with a tool or website they shouldn't be using.

However, once you pass that pool safety rope (you know, the one with the buoys that you aren't supposed to hang onto), a lot more responsibility falls on the students to behave appropriately. Being in the deep end also means that students can do more than they could in the shallow end. As a teacher, your role shifts from someone telling them to stay in the shallow end, to someone encouraging them to try new tricks off the diving board or to touch the bottom of the pool. Just as with a swimming pool, you can see the inherent risks in doing this with technology.

Enhancement Ideas for the Classroom

In Dr. Puentedura's research, he found that most teachers and students immediately gravitated to the substitution or augmentation phase of his model when any new technology was introduced. Indeed, when we introduced iPads to teachers for the first time, one of the very first questions we got was "Are my textbooks on there?" For many schools implementing a mobile device initiative, this will be the preliminary step to get devices into the hands of students.

Although almost all textbooks are now available in digital format, they were not when we started. Even today, many of the digital textbooks are really just glorified PDF copies of the original text. Using devices solely for the sake of reading electronic versions of textbooks or doing digital worksheets is a serious misuse of their potential. That said, it is a necessary first step—dipping your toe in the pool with technology. So although we don't want the learning to stop there, it's always encouraging to see teachers thinking in that vein.

For the next part of this chapter, I'm going to share three examples of both enhancement and transformative thinking about learning with mobile devices. Many of these examples are pulled from classrooms in my district or from districts I have visited over the years. Although I delineated the difference between elementary and secondary in the previous chapters, I'm not going to do that in these examples, and here's the reason: An idea that I share from an elementary classroom could easily be adapted or changed for the secondary classroom with some slight tweaks to content or expectations. The same can be said for a secondary lesson or concept being used at the elementary level.

Remember that at the Enhancement level, the technology is really enhancing the learning activity taking place. In some ways you can do the same activity without technology, but using mobile devices might create a slight uptick in engagement, interaction, and outcomes. With that out of the way, let's look at some examples.

Enhancement Ideas

1. Reading

As I stated earlier, one of the most common and natural ways to introduce learning with mobile devices with students is reading online. Let me start off by saying I believe that reading a physical book is still a valuable learning experience and should be a part of every home and classroom. While in some ways reading a digital book is directly substitutive (you could have students read a regular paper book), there are some features of ebooks that raise the level of learning to that of augmentation.

For example, many ebook applications allow students to highlight a word and have it defined, or read back to them to teach the pronunciation. This is a powerful tool not only for early readers in elementary school, but also for students taking on harder-to-understand text (like Shakespeare) at the secondary level. Having the book give you some context or understanding while you read it can be powerful.

Figure 6.2 Shakespeare digital book from The New Book Press. Image courtesy of Alexander Parkerand.

The latest-generation digital texts (not the glorified PDFs I mentioned earlier) even have interactive components built into the book itself to check for understanding. A recent example we've had some success with is the series of Shakespeare books produced by The New Book Press (see Figure 6.2). In this series of books, students can not only read the text on half the pages, but also watch it acted out by professional actors on the other half of the page. There are also ways to interact with the text and pull up references to certain words used by the Bard throughout his series of classics. Talk about the ultimate context experience!

2. Note-Taking and Reflection

Another great way to introduce mobile devices into your classroom is to have students use them as a tool for taking notes and reflecting on their learning. While note-taking can be done with pencil and paper, there are some limits to those notes without technology. However, we've seen examples where students (and adults) prefer to write and take notes on paper, and in some cases that may actually be better for retention, as suggested by this 2014 article from *Scientific American* magazine: http://mrhook.it/notes.

Of course, the downside of this method is that when the notes aren't digital, they can be lost quickly. Since most devices come with a camera attached, encourage your students to capture their hand-written notes digitally so they have a backup if their notebook is lost or misplaced. Another suggestion for the classroom teacher is to be consistent, but also to allow for some level of personalized choice when it comes to note-taking. There are so many different tools out there, from the hand-written notes mentioned before to tools like Evernote or Google Docs that each offer their own benefits for the student.

Generally, I would recommend some sort of note-taking that is cloud-based and shareable. This way, if a student's device quits working, they can still access their notes online. Also, if there is a point during the learning process where the classroom teacher wants to see the notes (such as in secondary science classrooms), the student will have an easy way to share those with their teacher or other classmates.

One last point I'll make in this area is that note-taking in a visual form can also be powerful for learning and retention. The concept of "sketchnotes" has been a growing trend among professionals and really can help a visual learner with reflection and retention. I've started doing this as professional practice as well, and although my art still leaves something to be desired, I tend to remember more of what was said during a talk or keynote, as seen in Figure 6.3. For point of reference I used the app "Paper by 53" (www.fiftythree.com)

Figure 6.3 My sketchnote reflection of Adam Bellow's ICE 2016 keynote address.

here for my sketchnote of Adam Bellow's keynote at the ICE conference in February 2016.

3. Presenting Ideas

One of the last examples I'll share really starts to shift thinking from just enhancement to transformation. Although making presentations in Microsoft PowerPoint to share your information has been around for decades, there are now many more mediums to use to display your knowledge and under-standing of a concept. In some ways, you could consider the idea of students presenting information in a presentation tool to be substitutive. Couldn't they also display their information on one of those trifold poster boards made famous by science fairs across the country?

Where presentations start to cross over into augmentation (and ultimately to the transformative level) is when the technology allows for tasks that you couldn't do on a poster board, and even some tasks that were previously impossible without technology. I'll give you one of my favorite examples here: explaining Latin with Minecraft.

A couple of years into our iPad initiative, we saw some immediate benefits for students presenting their understanding. Using Keynote for the iPad, students could create simple presentations explaining their thinking or knowledge of a learning objective. In Natalie Cannon's Latin class, one student wanted to try something a little different.

The task was to create a presentation (presumably on PowerPoint or Keynote) that outlined and explained the various parts of a Roman bath house in Latin. This assignment could have been done by the student in a couple of hours, but this student wanted to dive deeper and use a tool that he had become very comfortable with: Minecraft.

In case you've been living under a rock for the last several years, Minecraft is an interactive world where users can create and destroy materials one block at a time. This particular student wanted to re-create the Roman bath house to scale and then screen record his creation and do a voiceover in complete Latin. While the original task (presenting parts of a Roman bath house in Latin) could have been done without technology, the way in which this student used technology to enhance both his understanding and that of the students (and teacher) in his class begins to demonstrate how technology can be transformative when used in the right way.

Workflow Discussion

Before we dive into some transformative ideas, one of the major differences between these two areas of learning with mobile devices tends to be the workflow. Teaching and learning in the enhancement realm very much mirrors what teaching and learning looks like in a non–mobile device classroom. The teacher is still the primary source of interaction with the students, and tasks to be completed must flow back and forth with her or him. Here's an example:

1. The teacher assigns a paper or worksheet to students and distributes this to them by asking one student to take a paper and pass the rest back.

2. Students complete the assignment using their pencils and then turn the paper back to the teacher.

3. The teacher then grades the assignment or gives some level of feedback for the student to continue working on it and hands it back to the student.

This "typical" workflow scenario would also work well in a classroom that enhances with technology, with a few minor tweaks and in some cases with the addition of a content or learning management system (LMS). In this new enhanced scenario, we see some subtle changes, but the teacher is still the focal point:

1. The teacher assigns an electronic worksheet or project to the students either via email or through some sort of learning management system where assignments can be accessed by students.

2. Students complete the assignment or task and then submit their work to the teacher to review via email, the LMS, or some sort of shared folder system such as Google Drive.

3. The teacher than grades the assignment or gives some level of feedback to the student digitally.

4. The students can then make some adjustments with the teacher's feedback and share back the final revisions.

There isn't much difference between these two scenarios, and for many reasons, that's why major LMS systems like Blackboard or Canvas have been so successful in the K–20 educational space. Those systems in some ways perpetuate the teacher-centric method of teaching with mobile devices (discussed in Chapter 4) versus a student-driven one.

Before I go any further, let me clarify by saying there are in fact times when this method of teaching and workflow is necessary. However, I do not think that you should use only this method of instruction in your everyday teaching practice, whether or not you have mobile devices.

Going Transformative in the Classroom

The third enhancement example, with the student using Minecraft, brought back memories of a similar experience I had in school, only with a different outcome. When I was in sixth grade, I was asked to do the typical "creating a step-by-step recipe" assignment. The assignment was to go home and create a recipe card based on the preparation of some sort of food item. (Step 1, take out the bread. Step 2, apply the peanut butter, etc.)

It just so happened that I had this amazing (and quite heavy) piece of technology known as a VHS camcorder. I loved making films and shows with this device as a child, and I thought rather than just making a boring recipe card, I would create my own cooking show!

With my dad as the cameraman and editor, I shot and reshot many different versions of my recipe for what I called "Carl's Famous Cookie." It was essentially a giant sheet cookie that contained sugar, butter, chocolate chips and oatmeal, but I digress. I completed the project and brought the tape to school. I asked the teacher to find the one TV/VCR cart in the school at the time (usually located in the library) and wheel it into class for my project. With my fellow students gathered around, I proudly shared my cooking show and recipe.

The result? Thunderous applause (at least how I remember it) from my class-mates! However, I then received my grade for the assignment: an "F." How could this be? I was being so innovative! Why did I get an F? The teacher responded, "You didn't follow directions." I was devastated. It would be the first and only F I would ever receive in my K–12 education, and it left a lasting effect on my 12-year-old brain. This assignment wasn't about demonstrating the steps of how to accomplish a task—it was about following directions. It wasn't about showing my learning—it was about writing down "Step 1—Take out a mixing bowl."

Figure 6.4 Carl's Cooking Show

I shared this personal story, because taking your classroom into the transfor-mative realm of learning means a shift from the teacher's mindset. The most important thing can't be following directions— demonstrating learning must also be matter. Here are three examples where I've seen the power of learning when the teacher allows the student to drive the learning in a transformative way with mobile devices.

Transformative Ideas

1. Augmenting Reality

Augmented reality is not a new concept in technology, but the introduction of mobile devices with cameras has brought it into the classroom for the first time. This book and the Easter eggs hidden within the images is in some ways transformative. I could have never done this with a book if I had written it five years ago.

In the classroom, being able to layer elements of augmented reality onto a project can add not only a level of enhanced engagement, but also an opportunity for students to demonstrate their knowledge and understanding of a concept in a variety of ways. In my state, we teach Texas history in fourth and seventh grades. With no national curriculum to follow, this is an area where we see some innovative teaching ideas for the application of mobile devices.

One such idea came about from a fourth grade team at Cedar Creek Elementary in my district. For years, they had done the standard "book report" on a famous historical Texan. Each student would write out the report on paper, and it would then be posted onto a bulletin board or displayed around the school.

However, once each student had a mobile device, the team began to think of ways to make these historical figures come to life. Because writing is an important component of fourth grade, they didn't want to give that up, but they did want to breathe some fresh life into this project. Enter the idea of augmented reality. Before posting their book reports on bulletin boards around the school, students were asked to dress up and act out their Texas legend. Then, using the Aurasma app (the same one used for this book—www.aurasma.com), the students would overlay their video on top of an image of their subject.

Almost instantly, two things happened. First, students had to have a much deeper understanding of the figure they were studying. Because they had to act out the part of this character for the camera, they had to pick up mannerisms and accents and internalize some knowledge of what this person did that was significant in Texas history—beyond what would be needed for a written report. Second, there was a level of engagement and motivation among the students creating these projects. They each practiced the video portion to a much greater extent because they knew these would "come to life" right off the page of their report. Dr. Puentedura's definition of Modification states that technology allows for significant task redesign. That's clearly the case in this example.

2. Using the Web to Create Awareness

Our students live in a world where accessing information on the web is the norm. However, how often are our students putting their learning on the internet? Creating a blog with a tool like Edublogs or Kidblog can be a safe and controlled way to start that process of having students publish their best work or share ideas. In some ways, just publishing to a larger audience than Mom and Dad can have a transformative effect on learning—but what if you used that platform to help with a cause or raise awareness?

Our Westlake Virtual Vietnam Project (http://virtualvietnam.eanesisd.net) has been a part of the learning culture in our English III classes as well as U.S. History. Students are given the assignment of researching a serviceman or woman killed in action from the Vietnam Veterans Memorial Wall on the National Mall in Washington, DC, and then tell their story.

What's immediately powerful about this project is that it causes students to think outside of their own "bubble" of existence. In a world where they may be transfixed by an Instagram post or a clever internet meme, they now realize there is a larger world out there. In the case of our high school students, they also see that many of these soldiers who died in battle were their age. Besides the emotional element of this project, students also must figure out how to contact friends, families, and next of kin, sometimes without the use of technology.

Through letters, emails, phone calls and faxes, the student then collects images and videos of the soldier for their final video story. Using a variety of technology tools (see idea #3, next), the student creates a short film that encompasses the life of the soldier and how they served our country. These films can often elicit an emotional response from both the family of the soldier and the student creating the film. With the power of the internet, video, and collaboration, the life of this soldier becomes a truly transformative experience for the student creating the project.

3. The Power of Choice

In Chapter 4, I shared the story of a third grade assignment on the solar system. Rather than telling the students to deliver the content on a particular tool or app, she allowed a level of student choice. Much like the example of the student creating a Roman bath house in Minecraft for Latin class, giving students a choice of medium can increase their ownership over the content.

Giving students some level of choice with their devices can be powerful for ownership, and it can also lead to transformative learning. Dr. Puentedura says that Redefinition is when technology allows for the creation of new tasks that were previously unimaginable. If you are a teacher who doesn't allow students any choice or say over the process of learning in your classroom, this level of depth cannot be achieved. That said, having too many choices can also stifle learning, so the teacher needs to act as a guide and mentor for students making their choice.

Ultimately, there will be times in your classroom when students are in different parts of the pool. The student or students who have earned a level of responsibility may be allowed to swim deeper and try some new app or tool that the classroom hasn't used previously. A student who is struggling or may need more guidance can stay in the shallow end for a while until he or she feels comfortable going deeper. Some students may need to stay out of the pool altogether. The bottom line is, with your students, don't think of technology as a goal or ladder that you need to climb together. Think of it as a part of the everyday routine of learning. Like a pencil, a pair of scissors, or glue, it comes with expectations and instructions—but try to not limit what students can create if you let them explore the deep end of learning.

CHAPTER 7

FORMATIVE ASSESSMENT

With all the possibilities of mobile devices in schools, many teachers are left scratching their heads over where to start. How do we make meaningful change happen in learning with mobile devices? As we'll see in Chapter 8, just letting students consume content on their devices is a waste of their potential (the devices, not the students). But if you're a reluctant teacher or a self-proclaimed "technophobe" who struggles with the concept of giving up some level of control in the classroom, how do you take that first step?

John Hattie, professor and educational researcher, has pointed out in his series of books on visible learning that formative assessments can have a marked impact on student learning. Some of his research shows a 70% to 80% increase in student learning when formative assessments are used throughout the lesson and day to gauge student understanding (http://mrhook.it/hattie). With the knowledge that formative assessments have more impact on learning than even things like class size and repeated practice, a teacher starting out in a mobile learning environment can use this research to help take that first step in integrating technology into their lessons.

What Is Formative Assessment?

One of the games I love to play with a crowd of educators is called "Love/Hate" (referenced in books 2 and 3). In this game, people move to one side of the room (the "Love" side) or the other (the "Hate" side) depending on how they feel about a particular topic. I usually warm them up with a light topic such as reality TV, but inevitably I ask them how they feel about assessment. Even though I never say the middle of the room is an option, educators tend to drift right in the middle of the room to show their feeling on assessment. There may be an occasional brave soul who claims to love or hate it, but the general sentiment from the crowd is that assessments are a necessary evil.

The Autopsy

The "evil" in this scenario isn't the collective of assessments—it's the dreaded, high-stakes summative assessment. Those stress-inducing bubble sheets of doom that keep Scantron (and many other big-name companies) in business and really don't aid in student learning. The summative assessment is often referred to as "assessment *of* learning." The student has already presumably learned the material, so this is a way of checking what they learned. I prefer to call them an "autopsy of learning," in that the student is generally long gone from the course by the time the school gets feedback on their performance.

With the student no longer in the course or grade level, it's difficult to help them with any areas they struggled in. Best-case scenarios dictate that the

scores be passed onto the next-year teacher as a way of investigating what ultimately "killed" the student the previous year. These assessments are the reason
why "data-driven" decisions are happening more often in schools all over the
country. But they don't actually help students learn.

The Prescription

The next type of assessment is formative assessments or "assessment *for*
learning." These assessments happen throughout the school day and are quick
ways of assessing student learning that allow the teachers to make adjustments
to instruction. Rather than an autopsy, teachers get more of a prescriptive
diagnosis as to what is hurting the child. They can then prescribe certain
remedies and remediations to get the student back on track. These type of
data-driven decisions certainly give more feedback to the student and the
teacher and can improve student learning in the long run.

The Lifestyle Change

The ultimate form of assessment would be self-reflective or better yet, an
"informative" assessment that actually informs the person taking the assessment on how to improve. These are assessments that the students actually
manage and self-regulate. People today use all types of wearable technology,
such as a Fitbit or Apple Watch, to data-track their activity levels and food
intake to help monitor their health. They do this so they can learn their own
data and make small adjustments to improve their diet and, they hope, develop
a healthier lifestyle.

Doing this same thing for learning allows students to internalize the learning
outcomes they need to master. These kinds of assessments can really be
thought of more as "assessments as learning." The student makes a self-assess-
ment to test themselves on how well they know the material, and then seeks
out the necessary improvements to get back on track. If the first two types of
assessment were an autopsy and a prescription, this one most closely resembles
that of a lifestyle change. Rather than having external influences shape the
student's learning path, the student manages and creates their own assessments and strategies to get back on track.

Formative Assessments Gone Mobile

I wanted to introduce my definitions and thoughts about types of assessments before moving on to introduce tools and ideas for using them in the classroom. All the tools and ideas that follow can be used in all three formats, but are most powerful when used as either formative or informative assessments in the classroom. Making these a regular part of the classroom routine not only improves student learning, but also allows the reluctant technology-phobic teacher an opportunity to take a risk with mobile devices and learning.

Open Feedback and Reflective Assessments

The average class size in our schools can range anywhere from 22 to 35 students. In that environment, it becomes challenging to understand the needs, struggles, and questions of every learner. Often, only the most extroverted or outspoken students speak up with their opinions on a topic or question. Putting mobile devices in the hands of every student means that there is now a conduit from the student's thoughts to the teacher's attention. Instead of only hearing from two or three of the bravest students, the teacher can now "hear" from every student in the room.

One of my favorite tools for this kind of open feedback and reflection is TodaysMeet (http://todaysmeet.com). This tool is a device-agnostic way of pulling in information from all the students in the room, and they don't need an app or a login to participate. A creative use of TodaysMeet that I've seen in action is a teacher showing a video on a topic and using TodaysMeet as a backchannel for students to express their thoughts or speculations about a particular part of the film.

One thing I will mention is that not requiring a login means that students are able to be anonymous, which could lead to some inappropriate comments. Spending a couple of minutes at the beginning of a lesson using Today's Meet about appropriate behavior and netiquette can help avoid the need to moderate students who are acting silly or posting things they shouldn't.

Another tool that is a little less linear than Today's Meet is Padlet (http://Padlet.com). This tool is also device agnostic, web-based, and requires no login. What makes Padlet a little different is the ability to sort and drag responses around the shared space. Students can also post videos, pictures, and audio comments. One of my favorite activities is using Padlet to ask students (and adults) to reflect on an idea or preconceived notion by posting "I used to think …" and "But now I think …" as categories of reflection (Figure 7.1). As you can see in the following Padlet sample (with credit to Lisa Johnson @techchef4u for the background image), the reflections are posted for all to see, but can also be rearranged.

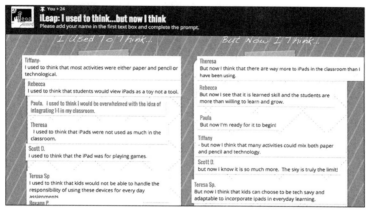

Figure 7.1 Using Padlet to reflect on learning.

Rapid Quiz and Polling Assessments

Reflective assessments provide some deeper insight into the minds of students through the use of an open response, but for some situations, the teacher just needs a quick check for understanding of a subject. Luckily, this market has opened up wide in the past several years as many software companies flock to replace the "eClicker" market of yesteryear. Now, with mobile devices, all students need is a link or join code to get into a quick assessment.

Before technology like mobile devices, this type of assessment could be given by students raising their hands or writing responses on a whiteboard and holding it up. However, in these situations, the data is lost the second the student lowers his/her hand or whiteboard. Although there are likely entire books written on the tools available for teachers in this area, I'm going to focus on three of the biggest players in the space and the advantages each offer when it comes to either a rapid quiz or poll.

Kahoot!

In 2014 while attending the SXSWEdu conference in Austin, I stumbled on a couple of very interesting Norwegian gentlemen. They were starting up a web-based quizzing system that was extremely easy to set up and run, but also competitive and fun. The guys behind Kahoot! (http://create.kahoot.it) have said their main quizzing tool will remain free forever and that they want it to be web-based and available to any school regardless of device.

I've seen an elementary music teacher use Kahoot! to have her students identify composers based on the music played during the question. I've seen history teachers use it to gather quick feedback on how much prior knowledge a group of students have on a particular subject. One of the most powerful uses of Kahoot! I have witnessed was when I saw a group of fourth grade students creating their own informative assessment using their iPads and the physical textbook (Figure 7.2).

Figure 7.2 Students creating their own kahoot for themselves and other students.

These students used the physical textbook to learn and rehearse the material of a particular chapter. They then created their own assessment of the content to both test themselves and to assesses other students' knowledge. When I asked the students what they thought about making their own quizzes versus having the teachers create them, they mentioned how empowered they felt. Knowing that other students would be taking their Kahoot! quiz meant that they had to provide the correct answers and that they needed to learn how to create answers that were close, but not actually the correct choice. In a way, they placed themselves into the minds of the national test creators.

Because Kahoot! is timed, the competitive elements in kids kicks in and engages them in the quiz. When we asked a panel of high school students "If you could invent an educational app, what should it have in it?" they all mentioned that having a competitive element like Kahoot! to engage the learners would be key.

Sometimes, looking for quick multiple-choice answers isn't the only type of rapid feedback you might want. Gathering the feeling of students in the room with a thumbs-up and thumbs-down can be useful, but polling a large group of students over the course of the day to give written feedback or thoughts can be challenging, especially without some sort of device to input all the answers.

Poll Everywhere

Using a tool like Poll Everywhere (http://polleverywhere.com), a teacher can not gather feedback from the students on a question, but the data can also be cleanly displayed in a variety of formats. Students can enter in complete sentences to answer more intense questions or select from a variety of choices to answer a survey. Using the "Discord" or brainstorm feature allows students to not only input answers but also vote up or down the ones they find most or least useful.

One of my favorite ways to use Poll Everywhere is to crowd-source answers to a particular question or topic. Figure 7.3 shows the "cloud" response I received when I asked an audience of teachers what skills they feel are most important for students to learn for the future. As they enter their responses on their phones, tablets, or laptops, the repetitive answers begin to grow in size relative to the number of times audience members have used the same response. It's always great to see the reactions of students, teachers, or parents as they watch their answers come to life and almost become a piece of technological art.

Figure 7.3 A crowd-sourced "cloud" responses using Poll Everywhere.

Embedded Assessments

I selected the tools just discussed for using assessment in the classroom primarily for three reasons:

1. Ease of use

2. Web-based (device agnostic)

3. No login required

A classroom teacher could create these quickly and replace an existing formative assessment or pop quiz almost instantly. For the next two major assessment tools, the assessment begins to transform into something much more embedded in the learning. In other words, it isn't just a one-off method of gathering data of student comprehension. These methods take a little more work from the teacher (or student) to create, but generally can be even more effective in increasing the learning capacity of the student as Hattie envisioned.

iBooks Author

When Apple created iBooks for the iPad, the thought was that students could now consume content digitally without the need for heavy textbooks. Although this did save paper, it wasn't necessarily transformative for learning. With the creation of iBooks Author, a free piece of software for the Mac

Operating System, teachers could now create and remix their own digital textbooks. More importantly, they could also now embed actual assessments into the book as students read.

This innovative way to embed assessments into the textbook is device specific (as of this print, iBooks can only be read on iOS or MacOS devices), and it has opened the minds of many of the main publishing companies to step up their game when it comes to digital textbooks. The days of looking over the PDF version of a textbook are now coming to an end. Now you can zoom in on an image, interact with widgets, and watch videos in the actual book.

With the content becoming more interactive and engaging for the student, adding an assessment widget can check for understanding while the student advances through the content. This doesn't require another tool or app either, as the interactive quiz is actually embedded in a page of the "book." Here's hoping this trend of embedded assessments continues to evolve as the ebook market grows and the demand for more digital content increases.

Nearpod

Nearpod (www.nearpod.com) is a tool that started out as a way to replace the stand-and-deliver teacher PowerPoint from a large projection screen to the hands of the kids. Moving through slides not only on your device but also on the students' devices keeps kids a bit more engaged and allows the teacher to see who is still with the class and who has dropped out and switched to a different app or off-task website.

While Nearpod began as presentation replacement, it's evolved into so much more. Teachers can now embed videos for students to watch at their own pace, focus students on a website or particular webpage, and even have students take a 360-degree virtual field trip of almost any place in the world. In terms of assessment, there are a multitude of ways to gather student feedback, from the traditional quiz and polling methods to a "draw it" tool that gives students a canvas to display their understanding of a question or problem.

Using the "Share" feature in Nearpod can also take learning to a higher level. The teacher can share other students' responses anonymously and even share the results of a particular question with the entire class. Students can then change or adjust their responses, discuss why they responded the way they did, and truly inform their own learning and that of the class as a whole.

Transformative Assessment

A tool like Nearpod lines up nicely with Dr. Ruben Puentedura's idea of transformative learning on the SAMR scale (http://mrhook.it/samr). Delivering assessment in that manner is something that could not have been done without the use of technology and in some ways wasn't even conceivable before the introduction of the mobile device. The teacher and student now have a variety of methods to convey their understanding rather than just bubbling in an answer on a Scantron with a number 2 pencil.

All of these tools allow for a wide variety of visual feedback. Posting photos on a Padlet wall or displaying a crowd-sourced word cloud in Poll Everywhere brings the data to life in many ways, but it is limited in the sense that it's purely visual. What if you could actually hear what a student was thinking when they were coming up with their answer? Being able to hear the process of how a student got to a particular answer would help the teacher see where an incorrect answer may have gone awry.

One of my favorite applications for this type of transformative assessment is Explain Everything (http://explaineverything.com). This app, which can be downloaded and used on almost any device, actually records the thinking and explanation from the student. A student could embed videos, images, websites, drawings and text into their explanation and then record their voice to dictate how they came up with a type of solution.

On the teacher side, this means you can see and hear what the student was thinking while processing the answer to question or problem you posed. This is not the type of rapid formative assessment I mentioned earlier, but it does allow for much deeper insight into the process thinking of students and how to help them make adjustments. Students can create and demonstrate their understanding rather than check a box or guess at a multiple-choice question.

All of the tools listed in this chapter have the potential to be used for many types of assessment. Integrating meaningful formative assessments with mobile devices expands the teacher's insight into the student's thinking. No longer will the teacher just hear from the one or two students who choose to raise their hands. For the first time in the history of education, we can now hear from every child in the classroom. We can make adjustments to our own lessons and instructions based on their responses, or, better yet, we can help them make their own adjustments toward their learning goals. That kind of learning environment brings Hattie's research to life when it comes to the learning efficiency of students in today's system.

CHAPTER 8

THE MOBILE LEARNING QUADRANT

For generations, the main areas of learning in the classroom have been the same: reading, writing, math, science, and social studies. These "core" subject areas of curriculum have been a focus of American learners since the mid-20th century. They were thought to be the essential curriculum necessary to prepare youth for success in college and the workplace. The manner in which these subject areas were taught mirrored the factory model method in which they were delivered. Content was passed back, row by row, as students repeated tasks and built skills over time.

While both traditional teaching styles and core subject areas have been slow to change to the modern world, the new area of mobile devices in classrooms is disrupting all of our previous ideologies around these sacred pillars of education. Repetitive tasks can now be gamified into forms that create critical thinking. Fact-based content can now easily be searched, opening up time to work on association and application of that information. Science and math have given way to STEM. Reading and writing are now being embedded throughout the curriculum in a more project-based approach.

That said, there is no magic bullet in education. Putting mobile devices in the hands of students will not change learning outcomes or test scores without some level of change in how students are being taught. Knowledge and application of the SAMR model mentioned in the previous chapter is a big step toward truly using the power of mobile devices in the classroom. However, it is only a step.

The Four Components

The shift in mobile learning begins with mindset (the name of this book), but also with rethinking some components of traditional instruction. These four components are:

I. Space

II. Time

III. Content

IV. Interaction

These four components aren't the only things involved in the day-to-day interactions in your classroom, but an awareness of how these are used with mobile devices in your instruction can greatly enhance what learning looks like in your class. Let's look at all of these components in detail and maybe some ideas on how to shift your thinking or practice in each area when mobile devices are introduced.

Space

I covered a great deal of this topic in Chapter 5 in talking about the learning environment in your classroom. The idea that learning can happen anywhere is not a new concept just because we introduced mobile devices to our environment. In the film *Dead Poets Society,* a film that took place in the 1950s when today's technology did not exist, learning still happened in a variety of places. Robin Williams' character Mr. Keating was far from a traditional teacher when it came to style and invoking emotion in his students. He also believed that learning didn't have to be contained within his four walls.

The students in his class got to hear the whispers of *"carpe diem"* from the ghosts of the school's past as they walked the halls. They could recite poetry while kicking a soccer ball to score a goal. They conceptualized the concept of conformity (or lack thereof) by marching in place around the courtyard. They shared their own interests and creations in the infamous cave scenes. What's great about those scenes in the cave is that someone is noticeably absent … the teacher.

Although this is a fictional film, the principles around space and where learning can happen can still be applied in the modern classroom with mobile devices. Hallways, staircases, outside benches, and the classroom floor can all be great places for students to carve out their own "cave space" for learning. In analyzing the use of space in your classroom, think to yourself, how often do I make my students sit in their assigned seats versus actually moving to a more comfortable learning space?

Time

When do you learn best? In the morning after a cup of coffee? In the evening when you've had a chance to unwind? When I ask large groups of students or educators this question, I usually get a large array of responses. One thing is certain—we all learn differently at different times of the day.

When I completed my #Student4aDay challenge (post here: http://mrhook.it/ s4ad), I realized that in some ways, the very structure of our school schedule limits the answer to the question of "When do you learn best?"

PERIOD	TIME	CLASS
1	8:40-9:30	English
2	9:36-10:29	Chemistry 1
3	10:35-11:35	Interactive Media
4	11:31-12:21	Lunch
5	12:27-1:17	World History
6	1:23-2:13	Geometry
7	2:19-3:09	Choir
8	3:15-4:05	Business Information Management

Figure 8.1 My student for a day schedule.

In going through my school day schedule (Figure 8.1), I discovered that my brain wasn't really ready for learning chemistry at 9:36 in the morning. In fact, when I took chemistry in college, I remember faring much better in the course when I took it in the afternoon. On the flip side of that, having English first thing in the morning was great for me and the way my brain processed that content. The experience of being a student for an entire day made me wonder, how much are we limiting student personalization based on their schedule? It also made me realize that mobile devices could help with this personalization—but more on that in a minute.

What is the largest university in the United States? Some may say Ohio State University (over 55,000 students). Others may claim Arizona State (over

73,000). They would all be wrong by a long way. When it comes to student enrollment, the largest university in the United States is the University of Phoenix with over 250,000 students enrolled in online courses and degree plans. While the traditional collegiate system has some level of flexibility in when you take your 3-hour class, it's still very much structured around a fixed time. One of the primary reasons why so many students are taking online courses (besides financial) is the fact that they can learn and create whenever they choose.

One more final nugget and then I'll get to my point here.

Have you ever used YouTube to help you learn, fix, or create? This is another question I love to ask a room full of educators, and the response is almost always a unanimous "yes." From fixing your washing machine to learning how to tie a tie, having a service like YouTube available to us means that we can learn whenever we want to learn and with mobile devices, just about wherever we want to (assuming good cell or Wi-Fi coverage).

Now think about your own classroom environment in terms of this second component of time. Do you allow your students to complete tasks at different times, or is it completely fixed? Is there any portion of your instruction or learning that you are putting online, as in a "flipped" classroom concept? Although sometimes learning does need to take place at a certain time and for a fixed duration (thinking about test taking primarily), we now have the ability to "bend" time through learning with mobile devices. We just have to open up our own practices to this concept and allow some level of access to other learning media (such as YouTube) in our classrooms.

Content

When I began teaching in the late 1990s, news media content was driven by three primary sources: radio, newspaper, and television. When a story broke, you watched it on the nightly news and then patiently waited until the next morning's paper to read about it in more depth. I had two significant moments in my life (and the lives of many Americans) when that all changed for me.

The first was when terrorists attacked our country on September 11, 2001. I was teaching first grade at the time, and many people were popping their heads into my room to give me updates. They had turned a television on in the staff room, and people would occasionally take breaks and watch my students so I could see the terror for myself.

That night when I went home, I turned on my computer and got on the internet. I discovered amazing tales of heroism told by the actual people there that day. I watched videos that had been made using camcorders (phones didn't have cameras then). But one of the places I spent most of my time was in discussion rooms on various sites. There was no Facebook or Twitter at the time, so this was a social place where people could go to get answers and find out information from sources other than the news.

The second significant event was the Boston Marathon bombing in 2013. In the 12 years since 9/11, phones had gained the ability not only to record video, but also to connect to the web and social media. I immediately began following the #BostonMarathon hashtag while watching the television with my wife. During the course of the manhunt, I discovered via a local citizen on Twitter that they had tracked one of the suspects into an abandoned boat. I leaned over to tell my wife, and then five minutes later the news broke on the television.

"How did you do that?" she asked.

"Twitter," I replied.

People were crowdsourcing the news rather than waiting for the news agencies to take the time to report it. Now, along with that instant content came the knowledge that not all online sources are reputable. Our kids may grow up in a world where access is instant and available at their fingertips, but they also are growing up in a world where they must check their sources and vet the content. Media content is no longer created by individual corporations to be consumed, it's being produced by the masses.

Consumptive Tasks on Mobile Devices

What does all of this have to do with education? When it comes to content in education, it's still mostly derived from physical textbooks, scholarly journals, or educational videos. Much of the content is still based on the core subject areas (driven mostly by traditionalism and standardized testing). It's curated and processed by corporations for our students to consume.

Mobile devices can now let this consumptive content take a much more interactive form if companies choose to produce it as such. Initial iterations of content on mobile devices meant glorified PDFs in the form of online textbooks. Still, at the beginning, mobile learning meant consuming content on a screen rather than in a book.

The latest iterations of ebooks now have interactive components such as built-in quizzing widgets, expandable images, interactive maps, and even demonstrative videos (like the New Book Press Shakespeare books mentioned in Chapter 5). Building these components into ebooks takes them from the substitution level of a readable PDF into an augmentation level of consumption. Being able to have the book define a word for you, play back the phonetic sounds, and even change the text size for student accommodations can't happen without technology and mobile devices.

The app marketplace was built very much the same way. A majority of the early iterations of apps were built to be used as consumptive tools and even, in some cases of poor use, digital babysitters. Teachers can place students on a math game app for 10 minutes and go work with other students who have more intense learning needs. As a former classroom teacher who struggled to meet the needs of all students, I certainly don't condemn this use of technology. It's more interactive and efficient than having students do the previous method of differentiation, which entailed handing a student a worksheet for practice.

However, if consuming content is the sole purpose of a device, then it's a waste of money for a school to purchase them. Don't get me wrong, there is some great value and cost savings in saving paper by completing substitutive tasks digitally. For many teachers that's where we need to start with integration—which is certainly understandable. Keeping consumptive tasks as a starting point for integration is fine as long as you acknowledge that it is a starting point and that with time and training, much more can be done with mobile devices.

Shifting from Consumptive to Creative

Just like the news media examples shared above, educational content is starting to shift from the corporation to the end user. More and more schools are taking advantage of open educational resources (OER) and online content to create their own curriculum. A teacher no longer has to rely on the scripted content of a textbook company and can now focus on getting students to master learning objectives rather than reciting textbook passages.

A resource such as CK-12.org allows teachers to download and remix a textbook into a "flexbook" where they can rearrange units, chapters, and contents to better meet the needs of their students. Rather than spending thousands of dollars on textbooks that are out of date as soon as they are purchased, districts can pay teachers to curate content that is needed to cover the learning standards. And the best part of that is, because it is digital, it can be updated regularly and owned by the district.

Of course, taking that to the next level would be having not only teachers create the content, but students. If you look at the learning pyramid (Figure 8.2), students learn best not by passively consuming, but by actively teaching and practicing. What better way to do that than having students create their own content based on their understanding of the content?

It's important to know that this concept of student creation and literacy isn't limited to the written word. Communication and literacy now take many forms beyond that. Visual, multimedia, audio, and video content are just a few forms in which students can be literate. Having a deeper understanding of digital literacy among a variety of media will not only help students as they enter the future workplace but also give them multiple ways to express their knowledge and understanding.

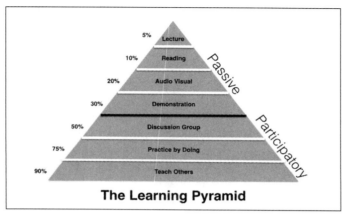

Figure 8.2 The Learning Pyramid.

In one of the scenarios I mentioned in Chapter 4 about classroom management, a teacher decided to give up some control to the students in her class. She let them decide what app they were going to use to display their understanding of a planet in our solar system. She decided it was more important that students demonstrate their learning rather than just staying within the framework of the lesson. She could easily have required that students read about a particular object in our solar system and take a quiz on how much they knew about the object. Instead she asked them to participate in their learning by creating a demonstration of their understanding using a variety of tools they had access to.

A tech-savvy teacher with a lot of energy and time can find a workaround to a file upload limit of 25 MB when students are trying to create and turn in videos, but for the teacher without that time and energy, this can be problematic. Rather than focusing on the importance of students demonstrating (and turning in) their understanding, the class is limited by the functionality of the LMS.

Realizing that learning can come in all shapes and sizes, teachers shouldn't hold themselves to the limitations of the LMS. In fact, with more things moving to the web and more apps interacting with other apps (also known as "app smashing"), students could just post a link to their finished product for teachers to look at. In fact, if every student had their own website and online portfolio, teachers could just ask students to post their learning artifacts online and then give them their grades privately.

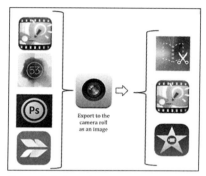

Figure 8.3 A modern workflow via Greg Kulowiec.

This new idea of workflow with smashing apps and posting to a URL can be complex, but it doesn't place technology-imposed limits on student learning outcomes as an LMS might. Greg Kulowiec shared an image (Figure 8.3) of what this new workflow might look like on an iPad. Using a variety of apps, students create content and then combine it into other apps before sharing the final product with the teacher. This enhances the student's digital literacy because of the variety of media being used, and it increases their knowledge and understanding because of the depth and energy they must expend creating the content for the teacher (and others) to view.

Does Workflow Allow Learning to Flow?

Workflow in many ways depends on the kind of content you are having students interact with. If the content is fairly consumptive, a standard learning management system (LMS) is the preferred method of delivery and exchange of information between student and teacher. One of the inherent issues with most LMSs is that their limits actually limit the variety of learning outcomes from students.

Interaction

In the modern workplace, employees can use a variety of resources and people to help them complete a task. If you are working on an important project with a deadline, sometimes asking for help or working with experts to problem solve an issue can benefit the project and enhance the final outcome. Although there are times to work in isolation and focus on the completion of the task, generally collaborating and interacting with others can breathe new life into a project or task.

Changing the spaces in the classroom to be more flexible encourages more meaningful interaction among[A students. Yet in some cases, even with a more adaptable learning environment, students are still placed in rows to complete more individual activities rather than interacting with each other and the teacher.

When I took part in the #Student4aDay Challenge (http://mrhook.it/s4ad), in the classrooms where the space was static, there was little to no interaction between students. In fact, most of the interaction was unidirectional (teacher to student). However, in the classrooms with more flexible space and student-created content, interaction was much more collaborative rather than isolated.

As with anything in life, there are times when you need to focus and work in isolation to complete a project. Unfortunately, in most schools that is what most time in the classroom looks like for students. In reality, just as in the workplace, students' learning can be enhanced by collaborating and interacting with peers to accomplish a common goal. When looking at space, content, and time spent on student learning, don't neglect the importance of student interaction.

Interactive Learning Challenges (ILCs)

In Chapter 8 of Mobile Learning Mindset book 3, I detailed the concept of using something called Interactive Learning Challenges (ILCs) to make professional learning fun and interactive. Taking each of the components of the Mobile Learning Quadrant and spinning them into motion is what an activity like an ILC does.

Students work in teams to move around the school and not only locate content, but also create it. They collaborate and delegate parts of the challenges that need to be completed within a certain time limit. Just as in the "real world," they are not bound by sitting in a desk or working in isolation. In fact, doing those very things is detrimental to their success in completing the challenges.

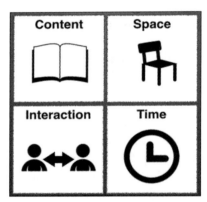

Figure 8.4 The Mobile Learning Quadrant (MLQ).

Infusing mobile learning into a classroom where students consume content in isolation in a desk at a set time of day is a waste in some ways. Creating flexible spaces that encourage collaboration to create content and an environment where learning can happen 24/7 is truly a thing to behold. Leveraging the MLQ (Figure 8.4) in this way can really enhance the efficiency of learning with mobile devices.

CHAPTER 9

TYING IT ALL TOGETHER

A s in every book in this series, it's important to see where each puzzle piece fits in the mobile learning initiative. Although the focus of learning is the student, the classroom teacher and learning environment play a huge role in effecting that learning. Teachers need to feel supported by their campus leader and the professional learning they are offered. The technology department needs to be dependable should a problem arise. The classroom parents need to be kept in the loop of any new changes or practices that might be taking place in the classroom that relate to mobile learning. And last, the district administrator needs to feel welcome to come and visit the classroom and must be aware of the changes taking place within the four walls of your learning environment.

What follows is a focus on each one of these groups and how teachers can leverage their place in the mobile learning environment to really bring about change.

Professional Learning

As a teacher, how many times have you seen this? You walk into a professional development session and are told repeatedly how learning in the classroom should be student-centered and not lecture-based. You are told about it so often that you realize eventually that all the learning you are receiving is lecture-based and very traditional.

Usually one of the first things that school districts cut are support staff. This generally includes someone who performs the role of instructional coach for technology. Luckily, with the internet and social media, a teacher no longer needs to feel isolated and can create a virtual professional learning network (PLN). Using Twitter chats as a way to crowdsource resources is a great idea for a teacher looking for other inspiring ideas. Jerry Blumengarten (a.k.a. Cybraryman) has curated an amazing list of educational hashtags for educators to follow (http://cybraryman.com/edhashtags.html). From #KinderChat to #MathChat, resources are being shared weekly on these online chats.

On occasion, your district may also let you attend some sort of professional learning conference about technology integration. If money or hiring a substitute is an issue, keep an eye out for an Edcamp in your area (http://edcamp.org). Edcamps are always free and usually on Saturdays. They provide a place for teachers to gather and learn as well as share innovative ideas from their classrooms. The grass-roots movement of Edcamps also makes them a great place to connect and grow your PLN to stay connected even after the camp has finished.

Larger state conferences such as TCEA in Texas, CUE in California, FETC in Florida, and TIES in Minnesota can provide a variety of larger-scale sessions and workshops. ISTE (the organization that is publishing this book series) organizes the premier educational technology conference in the United States.

With thousands of educators descending on this summer event from all over the globe, the variety of sessions offered is almost endless.

Of course, if mobile learning is your focus, you can find sessions on these topics at both the Edcamp and larger state events. My personal (and admittedly biased) choice for learning about mobile devices in school is the iPadpalooza event we host locally in Austin, Texas, every June (http://ipad-palooza.com—see Figure 9.1). This "Learning Festival" (we don't use the word "conference") is a three-day event that involves live music, amazing keynote speakers, food trucks, more than a hundred sessions on mobile learning, a film festival, and an APPMazing Race that pits teams of teachers against each other in the pursuit of glory, prizes, and ultimately, creative collaboration. Many other states like the feel of iPadpalooza so much that they have spun off their own independently run events as a way to get like-minded educators together in an event that encourages learning and even a little bit of fun.

Figure 9.1 My traditional opening vendor rap during iPadpalooza.

Although these events are inspiring and peer-building, simply attending conferences and learning festivals will not help you grow professionally without some action on your part as a teacher. As we'll cover in the final chapter, reflecting on your experiences and setting goals for your professional learning will help you take that learning and turn it into action.

Campus Administrators

Many of the innovations I've seen in classrooms around the country and in my own district related to mobile learning have happened because the teacher felt supported and encouraged to take a risk. In order for students to take risks and attempt something new, the teacher needs to do the same. In order for the teacher to take risks, the campus administrator must follow suit.

The campus administrator is the person most responsible for setting the tone of the learning culture in the school. When I've spoken with teachers who don't feel supported by campus administration, they often express a sense of isolation. They know if they try something new, they almost have to keep it to themselves. Sharing with colleagues in an environment that doesn't really support innovation can put the teacher at risk of ridicule.

"Why are you trying something new and making us look bad?" might be a complaint heard by teachers in a nonsupportive culture.

If a campus administrator isn't supportive of mobile learning, when parents and other issues arise, they might take a hands-off approach rather than helping with the situation. If they aren't encouraging the integration of mobile devices for every teacher with expectations and evaluations, then it's highly likely that many teachers won't even attempt to integrate.

However, if you have the opposite of that—an administrator who not only supports mobile learning but also expects its effective use in classrooms— teachers can flourish and feel free to push the boundaries a bit when it comes to student learning. One of the best cases for this is one I discussed in book 2, for campus administration.

The short version of that story is that when we first launched our 1:1 iPad initiative at the middle school level, we had two different campuses with two different types of leaders. One campus had a leader who supported the initiative not only in concept, but also in words. She would let staff know that the common expectations were for mobile device use, and that we were all in this together to integrate that use. The other principal told his staff that "the district" provided these devices for students and expected them to be used. At no point did he ever actually claim to support the initiative or set any level of expectations. As you can imagine, one campus took off when it came to integration and the other one floundered a bit until leadership changed.

It's always amazing the effect that one person in authority can have, not only on an initiative like mobile learning, but also on the climate and culture of the campus relating to teacher growth and sharing.

Parents

Using mobile devices in the classroom can present itself in two different forms. In one scenario, the district provides and manages the device used for learning (like a 1:1 or shared model). In the other scenario, the district encourages students to bring their own device (BYOD) for learning. Depending on which scenario your school employs, you might find that parents can provide a number of challenges and opportunities when you start integrating these devices into students' everyday learning.

Regardless of policy or scenario, it's best practice to keep parents in the loop about new and innovative strategies in the classroom. We once had a third grade teacher ask to use Twitter to help support the concept of summarization in language arts. At first blush, this seemed like a dangerous and misguided proposition. However, the teacher outlined how the student accounts would be monitored and controlled as well as the instructional uses of having Twitter in the classroom. She communicated those ideas with the campus and district administration, and then sent a letter home to make parents aware of what she was attempting.

With the support of both campus and district administration and clear parent communication, she was able to pull off what could have potentially been a tricky "sell" for integrating mobile devices and social media into a classroom of 8-year-olds. In the end, the students were able to learn not only better summarization but also early digital citizenship with actual social media accounts. (See Figure 9.2.)

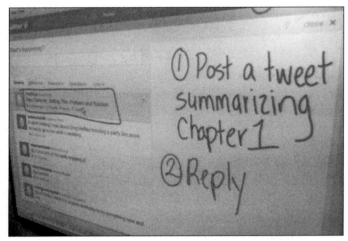

Figure 9.3 Example of a third grade teacher using Twitter to help with summarization.

Depending on the grade level you teach, there will be problems that arise from time to time when using mobile devices in your classroom. Students won't come with their devices charged, they might forget them, or they might get into sites or places they shouldn't. At first glance, these might be seen as technology problems, but in actuality they are behavior problems. Communicating expectations with students and parents at the onset is an important way to keep these behaviors from cropping up. We have used an iPad contract (one here by Lisa Johnson: http://mrhook.it/oath), and some schools even have students earn an "Internet Driver's License."

Students need to meet the expectation that they will be responsible in the use of a mobile device. That expectation needs to come from both home and school, which is why this partnership between parent and teacher is so important if you want mobile learning to really be meaningful and effective.

Technology Support

Once you've taken the dive into mobile learning, or any type of integration in the classroom, there are many inherent risks that I've already mentioned. One that I haven't is when the technology completely fails. When I've spoken at other districts around the country, I like to ask a poll question (using a tool like Poll Everywhere, mentioned in Chapter 7) about what one word teachers use to describe technology in schools.

The responses usually vary from "engaging" to "frustrating." In the schools where phrases like "frustrating," "unreliable," and "intermittent" rise to the top, I know there is an issue with technical support. Schools were not built to house technology for the most part. Many of them have been retrofitted, but an overwhelming percentage still don't have the wireless infrastructure to support a 1:1 mobile learning environment. If your school is a BYOD school, you have the added issue of dealing with multiple platforms and device types to integrate into the classroom.

These roadblocks can make even the most tech-savvy teacher call it quits. Cathy Yenca, the middle school math teacher I interviewed in Chapter 3, is one of our earliest adopters for most kinds of technology and applications. When we began using the app Nearpod a few years ago, it was extremely network intensive, and our bandwidth didn't really support it. It would regularly crash or stall out for students, and teachers would get frustrated, which would lead to them eventually not using it.

Not Cathy Yenca.

Cathy kept with it and not only worked with Nearpod on suggestions for improvements on their end, but also communicated with our network administrator and technology services team to see if changes could be made on the network side. Her persistence paid off 100 times over, as we now use Nearpod districtwide to help students with learning, and her own lessons are now featured in their store.

What would have happened if she didn't have that level of persistence? Or what if she had a technology services department that wasn't supportive or interested in helping her out? Unfortunately, when I go out and speak with other districts, I often hear about technology departments that only support technology and not necessarily learning.

As someone who spent a couple of years in a technology department building desktop images and virtual servers, I can tell you that every time the phone rings, it's usually a problem. No one ever calls to tell us how good the wireless is, or to let us know that the new app they are trying is working great thanks to our support or opening up of certain ports. As a teacher, knowing that before you pick up the phone or enter a work order can help you have some empathy for the technology department, which is often understaffed and overworked. The average private business has one technology support person for every 100 or so devices. The average school district has one for every 1500 devices.

For a classroom teacher trying something new, just as with parents, you need to keep an open line of communication with the technology department and be sure to always focus on the reason we are all in the building in the first place … the kids.

District Administration

The district administrator is the person who is generally furthest removed from the classroom—not only in years away from teaching, but also physically being distant from the classroom. In my years transitioning from teacher to technology department to district administrator, I've found that I spend less and less of my time in the actual classroom. Meetings, discussions, test monitoring, presentations to the board, and putting out fires all occupy the time of the district administrator.

Unfortunately, this leaves little time for them to see their actual "clients," the students. I spend some time in my first book focusing on the need for district leaders to be in classrooms more often than in meetings. As a teacher trying to integrate mobile learning in the classroom, you should remember to invite district leaders into your classroom when possible. Seeing their hard work in meetings and budgetary planning coming to fruition not only ignites their excitement, it puts a name with a face.

Personally, I have my set of "go to" teachers that I visit regularly, but I know there are many other great things happening in each and every classroom in my district. While I can't be in every classroom all the time, it helps to feel welcome from time to time. This can seem threatening to a teacher who is unsure of the technology or taking a risk, but if they are trying something that will help with student learning, I can promise you a district administrator will support it.

As a teacher, you need to feel that professional learning is meaningful and that you can grow from it, regardless of format. You need to feel that your campus leader is supporting you every step of the way, especially when you take risks. You need to have an open line of communication with the parents of the students you serve, not only about technology, but also about learning. You need to feel the support of a technology department that may be stretched thin, but is at least willing to let instruction come before anything else. And ultimately, you need to see district leadership taking an interest in what you are doing in the classroom when it comes to mobile learning.

Without all of these components working in synergy around you and your learning environment, it might be easier to give up. But don't forget that when adults give up, it's the kids who suffer.

CHAPTER 10

REFLECT AND SHARE

The amount of learning that comes with reflection is really remarkable. Recent research has show how much more deeply we learn when we reflect on what we have just accomplished, whether it was a success or a failure. For me, blogging is an outlet for reflection, albeit a public one. By putting my learning process into words and sharing, I hope that I will learn as much from my errors as the people that follow my blog do. Often when I was a classroom teacher, and even now as a professional who attends various learning events, I'm saddened to see that reflection is usually left out of the learning process. Often in my classroom, I would be in such a hurry to get from one chunk of content to the next that I would skip over the "What did we learn?" part of class.

Now that teachers and students have mobile devices in the classroom, they have a wide choice of avenues and media in which to reflect. The key is making sure that time for reflection is built into the learning process. It's fitting that the final chapter in this book (as in all the others in the series) is about reflection and how to use it for learning with your students.

Getting Students to Ask Questions

Do we become less curious the older we get? Research on how often we ask questions or wonder about something certainly points in that direction. The research has shown that students' ability to ask questions begins to taper off at around the age of 4. The average 4-year-old asks 200 curiosity-based questions or wonderings a day. Compare that to the average 14-year-old, who asks between 0 and 2 questions or wonderings a day. There is a correlation between curiosity and questioning. The research goes on to show an inverse correlation: when we increase the reading, writing, and other content "fed" to our students, they tend to "crave" asking questions less and less (Figure 10.1).

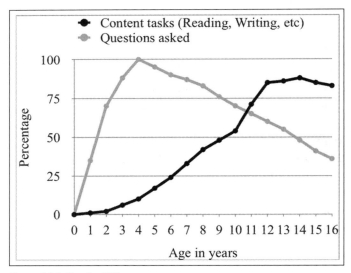

Figure 10.1 Caption???

Seth Godin says that rather than having students find answers to their questions at the back of the book, we need to get them to ask interesting questions and solve problems they're curious about. We also need to be OK if they get the answer wrong sometimes. Before diving into the practice of reflection, it's important to encourage curiosity and questioning in class, so that the reflections on those wonderings have meaning.

Reflecting in Class with Students

Part of encouraging reflection with your students is by modeling it yourself. Not every teacher wants to have a published blog or online journal, but even letting your students see you take notes in your favorite moleskin notebook or maybe jot down some notes or reflective thoughts on a white board encourages them to do the same. Some basic reflective questions might be:

- What did we learn from this?

- How could we have done this differently?

- How would we best share what we learned with others?

- Is there still something you are wondering?

The answers to these questions give you valuable feedback as a teacher. As a class, you can choose to either revisit a topic or leave it unresolved for a later date. Adding a digital component to reflection and scaffolding that throughout your class time will make this seem less like an "event" and more like a natural part of the learning process.

Exit Tickets

Mobile devices give you the ability to hear and see what students are thinking, if you employ them with the right teaching tools. As mentioned in Chapter 7 on formative assessment, using a tool like padlet.com can provide an avenue for quick reflection and an exit ticket. Sometimes this can be an outgoing thought on a particular topic, in class or a final viewpoint or vote for one side of a historical argument. One way I've used it with both youth and adult learners is to help me guide the next day's lesson—I ask, "What's something you want to learn about?" (See Figure 10.2.)

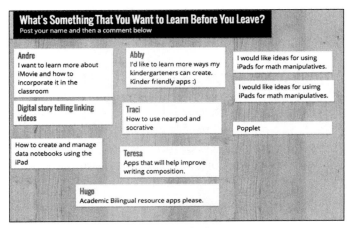

What's Something That You Want to Learn Before You Leave?
Post your name and then a comment below

Andre
I want to learn more about iMovie and how to incorporate it in the classroom

I would like ideas for using iPads for math manipulatives.

Abby
I'd like to learn more ways my kindergarteners can create. Kinder friendly apps :)

I would like ideas for usimg iPads for math manipulatives.

Digital story telling linking videos

Traci
How to use nearpod and socrative

Popplet

How to create and manage data notebooks using the iPad

Teresa
Apps that will help improve writing composition.

Hugo
Academic Bilingual resource apps please.

Figure 10.2 Using Padlet to reflect and inform.

Other tools like Today's Meet, Poll Everywhere, a Google Form, or any other application that allows for open response can be used to embed reflection throughout the lesson. This steers the learning in the right direction and helps students internalize reflection as part of the learning process.

Long-Form Reflection

Sometimes, reflection needs to be a little more in-depth than a simple exit ticket. You really want the students to think about the various stages of the learning process when going through an assignment, and identify areas of struggle and strength. Mobile devices give you an instant writing pad that, once it becomes digital, can take many different forms. Having a digital reflection means that it can be saved, shared, archived, or published as a portfolio of work for others to see.

As I've mentioned before, I'm a big fan of blogs for this purpose, but I know that sometimes the tool has to be adapted to the objective. Writing a blog means that you are publishing to a global audience. While that also means that you'll have authentic feedback, it could shape the vision of your reflection, as you might curve your thinking because of the very public audience who will be reading your words. Keeping an unpublished portfolio of work or an interactive notebook might be the best first step for teachers trying to increase the amount of authentic reflection happening in their classes, before moving to a blog format.

Video Reflection

Although the written word is still the dominant source of content in the world, there has been a significant shift toward video in the past few years. More than 300 hours of videos are now uploaded to YouTube every minute. Although many of these videos may be about cats, there are also some great reflections and opportunities for students to share their voices.

One of my favorite (though heartbreaking) examples of this happened with one of our Westlake High School students in his senior year. On December 6, 2011, while having a site visit and other important meetings about the state of our iPad program (it was in its first year back then), I happened on a student struggling to breathe in the hallway. He immediately lay down as his skin started to turn purple and for a short while, he actually died. It turned out that he suffered from a rare condition that occasionally stopped his heart from beating. The nurse on hand came and worked on resuscitating him. Eventually paramedics arrived and brought him back to life.

I was left personally shaken by the experience, as it served as a grim reminder that life is precious and you never know when your time will come. As I was reflecting on this event a few weeks later, I received an email from my superintendent that would later influence much of what I believe in education.

The email landed in my inbox on Christmas Day of 2011 and was merely titled "Westlake Student Video." My mind immediately began to race and turn toward negative thoughts—"Oh, no, someone used their device to post some inappropriate video, and now I'm in trouble for supporting this." Even though I was confident that our mobile learning project was of great value for learning, these fears and doubts still crept into my mind now and then.

As I began to watch the video, I noticed two things. For one, I recognized this student. The other thing I noticed was the number of views the video had … over 5 million. The video had been made by that very student I had seen collapse in the halls just a few weeks earlier.

Figure 10.3 Ben Breedlove sharing his message via video.

His name was Ben Breedlove, and his video was a reflection on his own life and the struggles he had with dealing with a very rare heart condition told very eloquently with index cards. (See the video here: http://mrhook.it/ben.) When I saw him show the card about that fateful day on December 6th (Figure 10.3), chills began to go down my spine. I then realized why his video had so many views. Ben had posted this video reflection exactly 5 days before he passed away.

While his story still brings tears to my eyes, it has always left a powerful impression on me. By choosing to share his reflection, he was able to inspire hundreds and thousands of other teens do the same (do a search for "Ben Breedlove" in YouTube and you'll see many other kids doing a similar reflection). His life may have ended, but his message persisted and continues to inspire many to this day, myself included.

His video reinforced three of my beliefs:

1. Reflection is important to capture in some format.

2. You should always make time for reflection.

3. It's important to give time to hear students' voice.

Using a simple technique like turning your phone camera on yourself can capture so much in just a few short minutes. Although videos can take up quite a bit of storage space on devices, consider having your own students (and yourself) reflect using video as part of that reflection.

Taking Risks and Sharing Failures

One final thought on reflection relates to taking risks. The recent trend in education is that we need to encourage our students to take thoughtful risks as a way of growing and learning. However, many teachers don't model this same idea of risk-taking in the classroom. There are a variety of risks in the adult world. On one end of the spectrum are risks that people take because of carelessness or just to be deliberately defiant. These types of risks are the most punishable (and rightly so). But that shouldn't prevent us from taking the other types of risks out there—risks that could have a positive impact on the learning environment. Taking an experimental risk that is focused on helping student learning can be still be perceived negatively if it isn't explained and expanded on.

When you consider trying something new in your classroom—with furniture, assessment, instruction, design, and so on—think aloud with your students about your predictions and goals in making this change. Just switching to more modern mobile desks to have something new in the classroom is a costly proposition if it doesn't result in some sort of meaningful change in your pedagogy. Giving every student a device so they can read their textbooks electronically is a safe start for a mobile device initiative, but if learning with mobile devices stays at that level of consumptive depth, in some ways it's a greater failure than not trying anything new at all.

Having the courage to step out and try something different to better student learning isn't really a risk at all—it's a necessary step to improving our end product. Using reflection within the risk-taking process can guide your next steps, help you set goals for final outcomes, and even help you admit when something goes wrong and discover how your class learned from it.

We no longer live in a world of isolation. Learning and reflection should at times be a shared experience. Internalizing that belief and then witnessing the outcomes will help you realize that really, the most important part of learning isn't getting everything right—it's trying in the first place.

ISTE STANDARDS

ISTE Standards for Teachers (ISTE Standards·T)

All classroom teachers should be prepared to meet the following standards and performance indicators.

1. **Facilitate and Inspire Student Learning and Creativity**

   Teachers use their knowledge of subject matter, teaching and learning, and technology to facilitate experiences that advance student learning, creativity, and innovation in both face-to-face and virtual environments. Teachers:

   a. promote, support, and model creative and innovative thinking and inventiveness

   b. engage students in exploring real-world issues and solving authentic problems using digital tools and resources

   c. promote student reflection using collaborative tools to reveal and clarify students' conceptual understanding and thinking, planning, and creative processes

   d. model collaborative knowledge construction by engaging in learning with students, colleagues, and others in face-to-face and virtual environments

2. Design and Develop Digital-Age Learning Experiences and Assessments

Teachers design, develop, and evaluate authentic learning experiences and assessments incorporating contemporary tools and resources to maximize content learning in context and to develop the knowledge, skills, and attitudes identified in the ISTE Standards for Students. Teachers:

a. design or adapt relevant learning experiences that incorporate digital tools and resources to promote student learning and creativity

b. develop technology-enriched learning environments that enable all students to pursue their individual curiosities and become active participants in setting their own educational goals, managing their own learning, and assessing their own progress

c. customize and personalize learning activities to address students' diverse learning styles, working strategies, and abilities using digital tools and resources

d. provide students with multiple and varied formative and summative assessments aligned with content and technology standards and use resulting data to inform learning and teaching

3. Model Digital-Age Work and Learning

Teachers exhibit knowledge, skills, and work processes representative of an innovative professional in a global and digital society. Teachers:

a. demonstrate fluency in technology systems and the transfer of current knowledge to new technologies and situations

b. collaborate with students, peers, parents, and community members using digital tools and resources to support student success and innovation

c. communicate relevant information and ideas effectively to students, parents, and peers using a variety of digital-age media and formats

d. model and facilitate effective use of current and emerging digital tools to locate, analyze, evaluate, and use information resources to support research and learning

4. Promote and Model Digital Citizenship and Responsibility

Teachers understand local and global societal issues and responsibilities in an evolving digital culture and exhibit legal and ethical behavior in their professional practices. Teachers:

a. advocate, model, and teach safe, legal, and ethical use of digital information and technology, including respect for copyright, intellectual property, and the appropriate documentation of sources

b. address the diverse needs of all learners by using learner-centered strategies and providing equitable access to appropriate digital tools and resources

c. promote and model digital etiquette and responsible social interactions related to the use of technology and information

d. develop and model cultural understanding and global awareness by engaging with colleagues and students of other cultures using digital-age communication and collaboration tools

5. Engage in Professional Growth and Leadership

Teachers continuously improve their professional practice, model lifelong learning, and exhibit leadership in their school and professional community by promoting and demonstrating the effective use of digital tools and resources. Teachers:

a. participate in local and global learning communities to explore creative applications of technology to improve student learning

b. exhibit leadership by demonstrating a vision of technology infusion, participating in shared decision making and community building, and developing the leadership and technology skills of others

    c. evaluate and reflect on current research and professional practice on a regular basis to make effective use of existing and emerging digital tools and resources in support of student learning

    d. contribute to the effectiveness, vitality, and self-renewal of the teaching profession and of their school and community

REFERENCES

Baer, D. (2013). Your office's fluorescent lights really are draining your will to work [Web log post]. Retrieved from http://www.fastcompany.com/3005976/your-offices-fluorescent-lights-really-are-draining-your-will-work

Blumengarten, J. (n.d.) Some educational hashtags [Web log post]. Retrieved from http://cybraryman.com/edhashtags.html

Berger, W. (2014). *A more beautiful question: The power of inquiry to spark breakthrough ideas.* New York, NY: Macmillan Higher Education.

Berwyn School District 100. (2016). *Pershing Elementary School website.* Retrieved from http://pes.bsd100.org

Common Sense. (2016). http://commonsense.org

Common Sense Media. (2016). *Introduction to the SAMR model.* Retrieved from https://www.commonsensemedia.org/videos/introduction-to-the-samr-model

Eanes ISD. (2014a). *Flexible learning environments.* Retrieved from https://www.youtube.com/watch?v=O_x4OLsfReQ

Eanes ISD. (2014b). *Hill Country Middle School iPad Oath as created by Lisa Johnson.* Retrieved from http://www.techlearning.com/portals/0/CarlHooker_devices_iPadOath.pdf

Eanes ISD. (2015). *Responsible use guidelines.* Retrieved from http://www.eanesisd.net/students-and-parents/enrollment/docs/WHS-RUG

Gensler. (2008). *Workplace survey 2008.* Retrieved from http://www.gensler.com/uploads/document/126/file/2008_Gensler_Workplace_Survey_US_09_30_2009.pdf

Hasbrouck, L., & Koch, C. (2013). *Exploring the link between physical activity, fitness and cognitive function.* Retrieved from http://www.isbe.net/epe/pdf/ reports-webinars/iphi-epetf-rpt0313.pdf

Hattie, J. (2012). *Visible learning for teachers: Maximizing impact on learning.* Retrieved from http://www.tdschools.org/wp-content/uploads/2013/08/ The+Main+Idea+-+Visible+Learning+for+Teachers+-+April+2013.pdf

Hooker, C. (2013a). Taking a dip in the SAMR swimming pool [Web log post]. Retrieved from http://hookedoninnovation.com/2013/12/10/ taking-a-dip-in-the-samr-swimming-pool/

Hooker, C. (2013b). The obituary of the student desk 1887-2013 [Web log post]. Retrieved from https://hookedoninnovation.com/2013/08/23/ the-obituary-of-the-student-desk-1887-2013/

Hooker, C (2014a). Eye-opening reflections on the #Student4aDay challenge [Web log post]. Retrieved from https://hookedoninnovation.com/2014/12/05/ eye-opening-reflections-on-the-student4aday-challenge/

Hooker, C. (2014b). The best app for monitoring students [Web log post]. Retrieved from http://hookedoninnovation.com/2014/02/24/ the-best-app-for-monitoring-students/

iPadpalooza. (2016). *iPadpalooza Learning Festival in Austin.* Retrieved from http://ipadpalooza.com

Johnson, L. (2013). The Eanes ISD WIFI Project—What do student projects look like in a 1:1? Retrieved from http://eaneswifi.blogspot.com/2013/10/what-do-student-projects-look-like-in-11.html

Lombardo, R. (2016). *Making digital citizenship authentic through PBL* [Web log post]. Retrieved from http://www.talkingheadstechnology.com/2016/02/ making-digital-citizenship-authentic.html

Maine Department of Education. (2016). *Maine Learning Technology Initiative.* Retrieved from http://www.maine.gov/doe/mlti/

May, C. (2014). A learning secret: Don't take notes with a laptop. *Scientific American*. Retrieved from http://www.scientificamerican.com/article/a-learning-secret-don-t-take-notes-with-a-laptop/

Puentadura, R. (n.d.). The SAMR model [Web log post]. Retrieved from http://www.hippasus.com/rrpweblog/

Westlake High School. (2015). *Student iPad orientation.* Retrieved from https://www.bulbapp.com/u/ipad-set-up-essentials

Westlake High School. (2016). *Virtual Vietnam project.* Retrieved from http://virtualvietnam.eanesisd.net

Wood, W. (2014, August). *Habits in everyday life: How to form good habits and change bad ones.* Paper presented at the 122nd annual convention of the American Psychological Association, Washington, DC.